Advertisements are taken in
by the Printers hereof . . . and by
the Men that carry the News

Northampton Mercury, May 2, 1720

THE MEN THAT
CARRY
THE NEWS

Advertisements are taken in
by the Printers hereof . . . and by
the Men that carry the News

Northampton Mercury, May 2, 1720

THE MEN THAT CARRY THE NEWS

A History of
United Newspapers Limited
by

GUY SCHOFIELD

LONDON:
THE CRANFORD PRESS
1975

Designed by
Ruari McLean Associates
Dollar, Scotland

Set and printed by the Leagrave Press
Luton and London for the Publishers
The Cranford Press
23–27 Tudor Street
London EC4Y OHR

ISBN 0 904 50800 5

CONTENTS

ILLUSTRATIONS

The following MEDICINES *are also fold by the Printer hereof, and the Men that carry this News, as also by the Bookfellers before-mention'd.*

Betton's Only True BRITISH OIL.

Which is an effectual Remedy for many Diforders incident to Human Bodies. It is an absolute Cure for all Scorbutick and Rheumatick Difeafes, for all old Contufions and Contractions of the Nerves, or contracted and withered Limbs, Strains, Ulcers, old Sores, all fixed and wandering Pains: It difcuffes Nodes; cures the Palfy, Lamenefs, Swellings, Inflammations, St. Anthony's Fire, King's-Evil; takes away all Blacknefs of a Fall or Bruife in an Hour's Time, and allays all Swellings that ufually attend fuch Accidents: It cures all green Wounds and Cuts, if fpeedily applied; it is an almoft infallible Remedy for the Rickets in Children; it is a certain Cure for the Leprofy, of ever fo long ftanding; very much helps to knit broken Bones, and is an excellent Antidote againft Poifon. Inwardly taken, it cures Ulcers of the Lungs, Shortnefs of Breath, Confumptions, Phthifick, Coughs, and almoft all Diforders of the Breaft or Lungs; it alfo cures Deafnefs to Admiration; it cures all Surfeits in Cows or Horfes; alfo Hardnefs or Stoppage in the Maw, the Maggots or Mange in Sheep, &c.

N. B. It will expel Poifon, heal the Bite af a mad Dog, and is an abfolute Cure for the moft obftinate Itch that has baffled the Force of all other Medicines. Price 1 s the Bottle.

A S   A L S O

Dr. Bateman's Pectoral Drops, for the Rheumatifm, &c. at 1s.

Dr. Fraunces's Female Strengthening Elixir, 1 s. 6 d.

Baron Schwanberg's Liquid-Shell, for the Stone and Gravel, &c. 1 s. 6 d.

(Publifhed under Sanction of the King's Royal Patent.)

Dr. Radcliffe's famous Purging Elixir, for the Scurvy, &c. 1s.

The true and right Daffy's Elixir, at 1 s. 3 d. the Half-Pint.

Bettons' Refined Oil, to take inwardly for Confumptions and Diforders of the Breaft and Lungs, at 1 s. 6 d. the Bottle.

Chafe's Balfamick Pills, at 2 s. the Box.

The Bottle for the Scurvy in the Gums and Teeth, 1 s.

Dr. Stoughton's Great Stomachick Elixir, 1 s.

Dr. Bateman's Golden and Plain Spirits of Scurvy-Grafs, 1s.

Dr. Boftock's and Squire's Elixirs, 1 s. 3 d.

Dr. Anderfon's Grana Angelica, or the true Scotch Pills, fealed with the Doctor's Head between C. D. at 1 s. the Box, round or oval.

A famous and infallible Cure for the Itch, at 1 s. the Pot.

Superfine Durham and Common Flour of Muftard-Seed: The Durham at 1 s. 4 d. the large, and 8 d. the fmall Bottle; and the Common at 8 d. the large, and 4 d. the fmall Bottle.

☞ *Obferve that the Names* DICEY *and* OKELL *be in all the Direction Bills with every Box or Bottle.*

Advertisement for medicine from an early *Northampton Mercury*

PREFACE

IT IS one thing to write the history of a single newspaper; it is another thing to attempt the history of a group which today consists of over 40 newspapers—mornings, evenings and weeklies —and eight periodicals. Each paper, each magazine, has its annals and cherishes its own traditions. Nearly all of them were in existence long before the birth of United Newspapers Ltd, to which they now belong.

How should I tackle the job? After some head-scratching and room-pacing I decided to adopt the analogy of a tree. In Part One I tell the story of *The Trunk*—that is, United Newspapers itself, the "parent" company formed in 1918, which holds the total operation together and governs its growth. In Part Two are stories of *The Boughs*, the individual newspapers, which are both sustained by, and themselves sustain, the trunk.

There are various kinds of boughs. Some are great limbs, celebrated and influential newspapers, and of course, heading the periodicals, the immortal *Punch*. Others are slender branches, small weekly newspapers serving small communities. Some readers may justly feel that I could have dwelt at greater length on what their records disclose, for every newspaper enfolds a people's history. I can only plead that I have had to be highly selective and in places must have done what sub-editors are eternally charged with doing—cut out the best bits.

Similarly I have only mentioned a few of the names that, on their merits, deserve to be mentioned; but it could hardly be otherwise short of producing a massive tome. For inevitable omissions I am sorry.

When the question of precedence came to be considered I decided that in dealing with our more venerable papers I would be guided by chronology rather than consequence. The first-born paper comes first. It happens to be a little one but we are all proud of it for it is the oldest paper with a record of unbroken publication in the kingdom, and, we believe, in the world. Therefore the little *Mercury and Herald* of Northampton marches ahead of the famous *Yorkshire Post*.

In this, and in what I have generally tried to do, I hope I have reflected the family pride and mutual regard which is so strong an element in the group—that unity of the many-branched which *is* United.

G.S.
1974

Stop Press

After the bulk of this book had gone into production came the announcement in the Queen's Birthday Honours of 1975 that a life peerage had been conferred on Sir William Barnetson.

I am just able to add this record of the event and to express to Lord Barnetson and his lady the cordial congratulations and good wishes of all who have the pleasure of being associated with him in United Newspapers.

G.S.

PART ONE: THE TRUNK

1

LLOYD GEORGE AND AFTER

FLEET STREET cannot offer another story quite like that of United Newspapers Ltd. It bears no resemblance to those woven about newspaper dynasties such as the Harmsworths, the Walters and the Berrys. It does not derive its impulse from the dynamism of an individual Beaverbrook or Thomson. Many men, differing in characteristic and purpose, have held the controls of United since it began its journeyings in 1918 and, in spite of some of them, it has proved itself to be a valiant phoenix, rising from the persistent mound of ashes that was deposited around it in its early years.

While it does not own a single newspaper published in Fleet Street it is rooted there; and while there are other groups, similarly rooted, that have also grown stout and prosperous, none has come out of such tribulation or endured such debilitating vagaries when young.

In days that still echoed with the departing thunder of the first World War a number of men who were associated with the war-time Prime Minister, David Lloyd George, bought the *Daily Chronicle* and *Lloyd's Sunday News* from the Lloyd family. The deal cost them £1,600,000, and they formed a new company which they called United Newspapers Ltd. The name has never been changed but it has sometimes been obscured.

At that time, and for some years to come, the *Daily Chronicle* was a power in the land. It maintained a splendid journalistic tradition. Its editors had included H. W. Massingham and Sir Robert Donald; the name of Sir Philip Gibbs springs readily to mind as an example of its distinguished editorial staff, and its literary pages had carried frequent contributions from Bernard Shaw and A. B. Walkley.

The paper had been founded in 1855 as the *Clerkenwell News* by a certain Mr Pickburn, at 35 Rosoman Street, Clerkenwell. (It is interesting to ruminate on the circumstance that, some years earlier, Mr Pick*wick* had also sojourned at Clerkenwell, beneath Mrs Bardell's hospitable roof just round the corner in Goswell Street.) By 1869 the proprietors decided to publish it daily and it became the *Clerkenwell News and London Daily Chronicle*, emerging ultimately as the *Daily Chronicle*.

Before then, however, it had been acquired by Mr Edward Lloyd of the famous paper-making family. Earlier still, in 1842, he had established *Lloyd's Weekly News*. In the history of journalism this paper, under varying titles which evolved through *Lloyd's Sunday News* to *Sunday News*, occupies a memorable place. It was the first British newspaper—as a weekly, of course—to reach a million sale and the first to sell itself for a penny. One of its editors was Douglas Jerrold, the friend of Charles Dickens, and it numbered Queen Victoria and Mr Gladstone among its devoted readers. Up to the beginning of the present century it was justly held to be a model of enterprise, particularly in the field of distribution. 'For the convenience of travellers who are crossing the Channel', it announced, 'boys will go over on the boats from Dover and sell copies on the passage'; also, 'where a tiny village only has to be supplied the agent may mount his bicycle and carry his parcel strapped on his back'.

Commendable activities; but the men who, with these two journals founded United Newspapers were interested in politics: their eyes were not so much on the efficiency of *Lloyd's Sunday News* as on the Liberal loyalty and Party potential of the *Daily Chronicle*. In the 'twenties, with a daily net sale of almost a million, it rivalled Northcliffe's *Daily Mail* and in January 1925, aiming to outstrip the *Mail* which had a Manchester edition catering for the North of England, the *Chronicle* also began to publish a Northern edition at Leeds. This was printed by the *Yorkshire Evening News*, one of two or three newspapers with Liberal traditions which United had by then brought under its control. They included the *Edinburgh Evening News* and the weekly *Doncaster Gazette*.

For some years all went steadily with United Newspapers. Its chairman was the Rt. Hon. C. A. McCurdy, a former minister in the Coalition Government, and among its directors was Major Gwilym Lloyd George; but his father, the ex-Premier kept a watchful eye on policy throughout the period from 1918 to 1926. It was a remote, invisible and little-comprehended control to those who handled the copy and set the type.

Then came a bolt from the blue. In November 1926 it was announced that the 'Lloyd George interests' were to sell United Newspapers to a group headed by the Marquis of Reading and including Sir David Yule and Sir Thomas Catto, two enormously wealthy merchants. They called themselves the Daily Chronicle Investment Corporation.

In the formal agreement, signed on July 11 1927, the sole vendor was described as 'The Right Honourable David Lloyd George. O.M., M.P.' and the sum paid, in cash and shares, was £2,900,000. It might be said that the 'Welsh wizard' got the money without altogether parting with the papers, for Clause 8 of the agreement ran:

> The Company hereby agrees with the Vendor that it will procure that the *Daily Chronicle* and the other news-papers now owned or controlled by the United News-papers (1918) Limited shall, so long as the Company has the power to control same, be conducted in accordance with the policy of Progressive Liberalism, in opposition on the one hand to re-actionary doctrines and on the other hand to communistic or revolutionary doctrines, and that consistent support shall be given to the promo-tion of unity in the Liberal Party and to the furtherance of social and industrial reform through the Land Policy, Coal, and Power Policy, Industrial Policy, Free Trade, etc., and other programmes of Liberal and Radical measures adopted by the Liberal Party.

This transaction triggered off a great rumpus over Mr Lloyd George and the Liberal Party funds. The high Tory *Morning Post* had a field day—or more accurately a series of field days. In a lead-ing article headed 'Unearned Increment' it congratulated Mr Lloyd George because 'we cannot see that there is anybody else to be congratulated' and, after drawing attention to the implications of Clause 8, went on:

If the purchasers should tire of these onerous conditions and decide to sell, then Mr Lloyd George comes in again, if he likes, since he has the right of pre-emption for the next ten years. Altogether it is as if a man should sell a dog—not necessarily a young dog—on the condition that it shall continue to retrieve his game or bark in defence of his property. The liabilities are sold; but the assets remain: we have seldom heard of a transaction more advantageous to the vendor . . . Whence came these riches beyond the dreams of avarice? On what capital sum are they the unearned increment? And does Mr Lloyd George hold this money as sole trustee, co-trustee, or absolute owner?

The *News of the World* estimated that 'a nice profit of about a million pounds' would go to the Liberal Party. It recalled that Lord Bute, who had held a big block of shares in United, had sold them to Mr Lloyd George and others only the previous year and 'must be kicking himself'. To the staffs of United Newspapers in London and the provinces these exchanges must have seemed like rather distant gunfire and the Marquis of Bute's contortions as unsubstantial as a dream. All they knew was that somebody else was ringing the till; their daily chores were unchanged.

On the formation of the Daily Chronicle Investment Corporation the chairmanship of United was assumed by Lord Reading—the Corporation, of course, was only a wrapper around United. In the *Daily Chronicle* he wrote, 'I am encouraged to contemplate the immediate future with firm confidence and keen anticipation'. The Press Club entertained him to dinner. Lord Burnham, who presided, offered him 'the freedom of Fleet Street' and the large company—which incidentally included General Sir Ian Hamilton—greeted him enthusiastically. Lord Reading made an appropriately modest speech as a new boy. 'I know now more of the difficulties than I did', he said wryly. 'I am beginning to realise what a complex machine the Press is'. Entertainment was on a lavish scale even for the Press Club. All tastes were catered for. The guests were able to enjoy artistry which ranged from that of Benno Moiseiwitsch to that of G. H. Elliott (the 'chocolate coloured coon') and the Roosters Concert Party.

In spite of this diverting revel the tokens seemed to suggest

that in the famous lawyer and former Viceroy of India the newspaper world had acquired somebody who would bring dignity
and lofty purpose to its future activities. But with the advantage
of hindsight one notes that, although Lord Reading spoke about
'ending his days in Fleet Street', he refrained from committing
himself in print beyond the 'immediate future', and one cannot
but wonder whether the Daily Chronicle Investment Corporation, as originally constituted, was anything more than a venture
rather vague about its own destiny or possible transitoriness. At
any rate within one year and one week after the completion of the
deal with Mr Lloyd George it sold itself. On July 17 1928, the
reporters, sub-editors and machine-minders employed by
United Newspapers woke up to find that the noble Marquis of
Reading was no longer their boss but a gentleman of plebeian
origin named William Harrison.

The world in general has long forgotten William Harrison.
Young journalists today have never heard of him, but in the
'twenties he crackled upon the scene beneath an aura of fireworks
more vivid than that which endowed Roy Thomson during the
'fifties and 'sixties. Nobody so completely justifies the cliche "a
meteoric career." He came, he flared, he went out. And when
he was quenched men stared for a space at the cinders.

William Harrison was the son of a Yorkshire farmer. He was
educated at Giggleswick School and Leeds University (Bachelor
of Laws) and in 1910 was admitted a solicitor. But the law turned
out to be only a medium towards quite other interests. If unim-
pressive in manner—he was described as 'dark and bird-like'—
he was mightily impressive in purpose. He was no shuttlewit[1];
he knew where he wanted to go. Through the London firm of
solicitors which he joined when he was 21 he interested himself
first in property and then in paper making, and by the middle
'twenties found himself chairman of the great Inveresk Paper Co.

In 1926 he invaded Fleet Street by acquiring the *Illustrated
London News*, the *Sphere*, the *Tatler*, the *Bystander* and other
periodicals which he combined as Illustrated Newspapers Ltd.
Then, nibbling at the provincial Press, he secured control of

[1]This word deserves to be brought back into currency. I found it in one of the
Paston letters, written from Norfolk in about 1445.

the *Lancashire Daily Post* and its *Preston Guardian* and the *Northampton Chronicle*. His purchase of the Daily Chronicle Investment Corporation—for our purpose United Newspapers —in July 1928 was the event that made him, at the age of 44, an important figure in the newspaper world. It was carried through 'on behalf of the Inveresk group' and in a statement to the *Daily Mail* Mr Harrison said:

> We purchased some three or four weeks ago a half-interest in the *Hull Daily Mail* and the *Grimsby Times*. We propose to develop the *Daily Chronicle* group in conjunction with our Lancashire daily newspapers.
>
> A new company will be formed in October to take over the whole of these interests. I believe it will be all to the public good that this new group, which will have strong Liberal interests, should come into existance. It will be a safety valve for public opinion.
>
> The newspapers under this control will resist any attack that may be made upon Mr Lloyd George, to whom the nation owes so much.

It will be seen that Clause 8 of the original Lloyd George agreement was still operative; the dog was still constrained to bark for its master, now twice-removed—ironically so, for William Harrison was, by conviction, a Conservative. He, or more strictly his Inveresk organisation, paid £1,130,000 in cash and £325,000 in shares 'in a new company to be formed.' On October 1 1928 the controlling interests in United Newspapers Ltd. and the Daily Chronicle Investment Corporation were formally transferred to Mr Harrison. Gracious speeches were exchanged; Lord Reading resigned and Mr Harrison was elected in his place.

By the end of the year he had completed his reorganisation plans. In his own words, he and his colleagues had decided that it was in the best interest of all that, so far as the provincial pro-perties were concerned, they should eliminate the subsidiary companies and have one company holding directly all the assets in the various newspapers they proposed to amalgamate. During January 1929 the operation was carried out. Subsidiaries such as Edinburgh Evening News Ltd. and the Yorkshire Liberal News-paper Co. (*Yorkshire Evening News*) wound themselves up and

6

became parts of the new undertaking, Provincial Newspapers Ltd. At its inception Provincial Newspapers Ltd. owned, in whole or in part, these papers:

Edinburgh Evening News	*Yorkshire Evening News*
Lancashire Daily Post	*Hull Daily Mail*
Eastern Morning News (Hull)	*Grimsby Daily Telegraph*
Hull Evening News	*Grimsby Saturday Telegraph*
Blackburn Times	*Burnley News*
Doncaster Gazette	*Hull and Yorkshire Times*
Hull Weekly News	*Preston Guardian*
Sports Mail (Hull)	*Sports Echo* (Leeds)

Sporting Pink (Leeds)

United Newspapers at that time was the *immediate* owner only of the *Daily Chronicle* and *Lloyd's Sunday News*. But of course United was, and ever since has been, in control of Provincial, even though for some years a large proportion of its capital was held by the Inveresk Paper Co. The two directorates have been almost identical throughout. It is well here to emphasise this reality because for a long time it was Provincial, as the actual day to day operator, which figured by name in the various provincial centres. By a tidying-up action in 1965 the situation was rationalised; United purchased the remaining 4 per cent of Provincial which it had not until then actually owned.

Little more than a year after the important Chronicle Investment transaction the clouds began to settle upon William Harrison. During the autumn of 1929 uneasiness about the Inveresk Paper Co. expressed itself on the Stock Exchange. Its ordinary shares, which earlier in the year had stood at £3.7s.6d. fell by degrees to fifteen and fourteen shillings. Something was wrong. The City found itself in one of its fascinating bouts of cerebral fever—and in those days there were still a few top hats to be seen perched on ominously shaking heads east of St Paul's. What was happening at Inveresk?

Amid this period of rumour and unease—to be precise, on November 30 1929—the first annual report of Provincial Newspapers was issued. It showed a gross profit of £256,340. The chairman of the company was Mr B. H. Binder (later Sir Bernhard Binder) a distinguished chartered accountant, the significance of whose presence will soon be seen. The other directors were

7

J. C. Akerman (managing), Sir Harry Brittain, R.W. Crabtree, Edgar Grotrian, H. Brent Grotrian, K.C., William Harrison, Ll.B., F. C. Macaskie, G. H. F. Nichols, Ernest A. Perris, Valentine Smith, George F. Toulmin, William H. Toulmin, Lt.-Col. James Walker, D.S.O., and George S. Wilson. The secretary was A. J. Snelson.

Quite a big hierarchy, one might think, for a venture setting forth amid looming difficulties, but the list reflects how various interests had been, perhaps hastily, gathered together. Mr Crabtree represented the important Leeds firm of printing machinery manufacturers which had a considerable stake in the *Yorkshire Evening News*. Mr Macaskie's family had been chief proprietors of that paper. The Grotrians were members of the family originally owning the Hull newspapers. The Toulmins likewise had been proprietors of the Preston papers. Ernest Perris was the dexterous editor of the *Daily Chronicle*, a man with a habit of breezing about on disconcerting impulse to the bewilderment of subordinates. The resonant-voiced Sir Harry Brittain, director of many companies and founder of the Commonwealth Press Union, was to remain on the Board for thirty years and, living vigorously, to celebrate his hundredth birthday on Christmas Eve 1973. He died in the Summer of 1974. Mr Snelson was to give long and devoted service as secretary.

Nearly all the others were to vanish like snow under the next springtime's sun; but three men on that original list should be noted carefully; they were destined to play leading roles in steering United and Provincial through the darkest hours. The first was the chairman himself, Mr Binder. The second was Mr Akerman, the managing director. The third was Mr Brent Grotrian.

Of these three it is to Akerman that the group owes the deepest debt of gratitude. He was one of those rare spirits in whom, by some mysterious gift of nature, apparently discordant qualities are harmonised. He was adventurous to the point of daring but he was also a calculating business man who sensed where the rocks lay. His insight was quick and his decisions were clear, and he had a zestful sense of humour that added charm to his company.

A glance at Jack Akerman's career shows exactly what sort of man he was. In his youth he sailed before the mast, did some farming in Australia, followed Cortes' wanderings for a while and, as a kind of incidental foray, won the amateur lightweight boxing championship of South America. All his life he indulged in extrovert activities—sailing, boxing, fishing, woodworking. He built boats up to 20 feet in length and he also made dolls' furniture. Back in London, about 1905, he sallied forth as a salesman for a new commercial art studio.

At the outbreak of the 1914 war he was on the managerial staff of *The Times*, whence he was seconded to the Merchant Shipping Department of the Admiralty. In turn he was Controller of Steel and Director of Admiralty Labour and Housing—an important post in the great battle with the German submarines. After the war he launched out into periodical publishing, and here he demonstrated his shrewd eye for the "new thing." His publications included the *Motor Owner*, *Modern Transport* and the *Advertisers' Weekly*. But they wanted Jack Akerman back on *The Times* and he returned as assistant manager.

Then William Harrison went after him. Akerman's friends advised him against abandoning the security and prestige of *The Times* for the unpredictability of Harrison's newspaper organisation, but he responded to the lure of adventure and joined Harrison. He could not have anticipated what was presently to befall, but the challenge when it came provided just those tempestuous conditions in which he was at his best, and it is no exaggeration to say that Akerman's expert knowledge, unfailing courage, and ability to confront adversity with aggression, were the chief influences that enabled United to emerge from its torments.

As already stated, Mr Brent Grotrian was on the Board by virtue of his family's interest in the Humberside publications which had come under Provincial's wing. His father, a remarkable and assertive character, had collected them during the last century when he was M.P. for Hull. Brent Grotrian himself had represented one of the Hull divisions for several years: he was accomplished as barrister, politician and business man, a strong, reflective individual whose quiet manner was rather deceptive. When necessary he had a salty twist of tongue.

William Harrison, it will be seen, was listed as a director in that first report of Provincial, but by the time the second report came out he was one of those who had disappeared. In fact his general eclipse was at hand. On the morning of December 19 1929 headlines in the newspapers quivered with excitement. 'Mr Wm. Harrison Resigns his Chairmanships: Inveresk Sensation Last Night', cried the *Daily Express*. 'Big Inveresk Surprises: Mr Harrison Resigns Chairmanship: Dividends to be Passed: Rearrangement of the Boards', proclaimed the *Morning Post*.

Although a crisis of sorts was not unexpected, the size of the explosion perturbed the City. The bang was to reverberate for months. The bank had stepped in and Harrison had stepped down. In the event it appeared that Inveresk was in debt to the tune of over £2,500,000 while United Newspapers owed half a million, much of which was in respect of printing equipment intended to modernise the *Daily Chronicle* plant. Meantime a committee had been formed under Lord St Davids to investigate the mess, and the Inveresk company issued a statement which included this passage:

> Mr William Harrison has resigned the chairmanship of the various boards in order to facilitate a rearrangement of the directorates, but retains his seat on the various boards.
>
> Pending such rearrangement, which it is proposed to make in consultation with representative shareholders, Mr B. H. Binder, F.A. of Messrs Binder, Hamlyn and Co., chartered accountants, London, who has been acting as financial consultant during the last few weeks, has consented to act as chairman *pro tem* of the company and certain associated companies, including the Daily Chronicle Investment Corporation, United Newspapers Ltd., and Provincial Newspapers Ltd.
>
> Mr J. C. Akerman, vice-chairman and managing director of United Newspapers Ltd. and Provincial Newspapers Ltd. will continue to hold these offices and the general administration of the newspaper undertakings will remain unchanged.

This story is not concerned with the subsequent course of the Inveresk Paper Co. and the unfortunate Mr Harrison has little more to do with it. The man was not sinister: he had been fondly over-confident, biting off more than a rational assessment would have deemed the dentures capable of chewing. Binder put the point in more orthodox terms in the 1930 annual report of Inveresk, where he spoke of his predecessor's 'policy of indiscriminate expansion.'

For a year or two Harrison went on protesting that he wasn't to blame, turning up at company meetings and writing circulars. During the annual meeting of United in 1931 he rose to speak amid interruption and, in self-justification, referred to the new plant which he had installed when in control of United. The chairman had to tell him tartly that he was not being blamed for having installed the plant but for having 'omitted to provide the money to pay for it.'

Millions manipulated unwisely—an old story, but like all such stories it bequeathed its quota of personal distress. Many were presently to be hurt but there was one immediately pathetic episode. One of Harrison's associates and most ardent admirers was Alexander Pike, a financier in a comparatively modest way. The Inveresk affair stunned him. His idol had crumbled. He no longer turned up at his small office in the City. When they refused to re-elect him to the board of Illustrated Newspapers he was heard to say, 'There is nothing left for me. I feel that I shall go home and die.' And that is what he did: he went home and died within a few weeks.

The story goes that a pensive William Harrison was seen loitering near the grave when they buried him at Barnet.

DISASTER OVERCOME

AND Bernhard Binder and Jack Akerman, together with Herbert Brent Grotrian, found themselves that cold Christmastide bleakly surveying what looked like the grave of United Newspapers Ltd. For weeks on end they sought a way out of the chaos left by the Harrison debacle. Binder and Akerman met daily in Akerman's office at Salisbury Square, working often until the small hours. At the annual meeting early in 1930 Binder pronounced a solemn warning that the financial situation was causing great anxiety.

It was not only the tangle of debts and absence of cash that caused this anxiety: it was the trading position of the *Daily Chronicle*. Editorially the paper was good, an alert and intelligent friend at the breakfast table; but economically it was in a bad way. Just what its condition was it is now difficult to make out; contemporary guesses that it was losing as much as £4,000 a week were probably excessive. The point is that United in its tattered state could not carry any sort of loss.

In a generous tribute the *Daily Express* was presently to say what was the truth of the matter: 'The news was handled brilliantly. The features were excellent, the sports side never excelled by any rival. But too many political and financial blows had been rained upon the newspaper's head. In spite of immense nervous effort the situation grew increasingly difficult.' Sir Robert Donald, a former editor, was to say, 'In recent years the *Daily Chronicle* has been struggling under handicaps which a competent staff could not overcome.'

These comments were made after the men at the helm of United had braced themselves to face the only decision that could save the company from total shipwreck. To journalists it was a heartbreaking decision. It was announced as follows on the evening of June 1 1930:

> On and after tomorrow morning, Monday June 2, the *Daily Chronicle* and the *Daily News* will be published as a single newspaper, under the title of the *Daily News and Chronicle.*
>
> Arrangements have been made for the transfer of the copyright of both papers to a new company whose shares will be held in equal proportion by News and Westminster Ltd. and United Newspapers Ltd.
>
> Control of the new company which will own and publish the amalgamated paper will be vested in five trustees nominated by the constituent companies.
>
> The first trustees will be Mr L. J. Cadbury, chairman of the Daily News Ltd., Mr W. T. Layton, chairman of News and Westminster Ltd., Lord Cowdray, vice-chairman of News and Westminster Ltd., Mr B. H. Binder, chairman of United Newspapers Ltd. and Mr J. C. Akerman, vice-chairman of United Newspapers Ltd.

Thus ended the *Daily Chronicle*, one of the finest, and in its heyday one of the most successful, newspapers ever published in Fleet Street. The men who signed its death warrant had no alternative if their other papers—those they owned through Provincial Newspapers Ltd.—were to be assured of substance on which to function. They had not been responsible for the sickness that made it inevitable. Others over a period of years had struck those 'political and financial blows' to which the *Daily Express* referred.

The fate of the *Daily Chronicle* is a classic example of a truth that is little understood except by professional newspaper men. A newspaper grows on its own roots, and when nursed by wise editorship evolves its own character. If you start binding it in directions other than those to which its nature inclines, or if you start grafting thoroughly alien elements upon it, it will languish— perhaps fatally. There are, of course, many examples of papers incorporating rivals, particularly among the older weeklies, but often this was a defensive measure—the incorporation of a moribund competitor's title in order to prevent anybody else using it. Ruthless handling and violent change are anathema to an established paper. Like a human being it has a nervous system and a heart. The two worst enemies it can have are the politician who seizes it and thinks he can make it holler his wares, and the management that tosses it about as if it were so much inanimate merchandise. They may appear to succeed for a time and the facade may even look good, but the years will reveal that it has grown sick at heart and tired of life.

Coming suddenly after only 24 hours of rumour in the Fleet Street taverns and, so far as the general public were concerned, out of a tranquil sky, the *Daily Chronicle* catastrophe stimulated a hubbub of debate and angry questioning.

It was realised that merging with the *Daily News* meant its elimination, no matter how they juggled with the title, which in the end became *News Chronicle*. Referring to earlier *Daily News* absorptions—of the *Morning Leader* and *Westminster Gazette*— the *Daily Express* commented, 'Another Jonah is in the belly of the whale.' Thirty years later the whale itself, suffering from a surfeit of assimilation, was gobbled into the belly of the *Daily Mail*—and much good it did the gobbler.

However, in 1930 that could not be foreseen; Fleet Street and the City were concerned with immediate consequences. Rival papers wondered what circulation they could pick up from the wreckage. 'You Can Always Get the *Daily Mail*,' said one placard, while another offered the distasteful pun, '*Daily Herald* Chronicles All the News.' Journalists and other workers were necessarily discharged, and if there was any touch of radiance in the murky scene it reflected honour on the journalists. There were instances of single men from the *Chronicle* refusing offers of employment on the joint paper when they realised that married colleagues' names were in the list of the condemned. At least one *Daily News* sub-editor whose job was not in jeopardy resigned in order that a *Chronicle* man could have it.

Inevitably the Northern edition of the *Daily Chronicle* ceased to exist and the editorial staff at Leeds found themselves unemployed. Here memory recalls a lighter episode which, if only in the most peripheral sense belonging to the history of United Newspapers, is perhaps worth its tiny place in journalistic annals.

A number of the workless Leeds men caught the train to Manchester and presented themselves, a melancholy deputation, at Withy Grove. Withy Grove was then the greatest newspaper complex in the kingdom, where Lord Camrose's Allied Newspapers poured out a stream of productions, ranging from the *Sunday Chronicle, Empire News, Daily Dispatch, Daily Sketch* and *Evening Chronicle* to sundry fiction magazines and racing sheets. And Withy Grove was good to the lads from Leeds; several were promptly taken on.

Nevertheless, having bravely ventured in their desperation across the Pennines, they found themselves in historically alien surroundings, and they clung together in a kind of White Rose ghetto. Among other strangenesses was the Manchester beer. On their Yorkshire palates it tasted deplorable; therefore when they planned a party to celebrate their good fortune in finding employment they wrote off to Leeds for a barrel of Tetley's best. It came. The party was held. And something happened which must be deemed unparalleled as happening to journalists. Almost before a second round of pints had been consumed the celebrants began to crumble; soon they were 'under the table.' Through the following morning's headaches they asked one another, with fervent anxiety, whether in so short a time they had lost the capacity to drink Tetley's beer? The answer arrived almost simultaneously from Tetley's. They apologised for having sent the wrong barrel; it contained an ale, exceptionally strong, which was brewed only for their draymen when off duty.

Mournful as the merger undoubtedly was, it gave United Newspapers, whose resources had almost disappeared, a valuable asset—a fifty per cent. share in the *News Chronicle*. Moreover the new daily began its career with the handsome circulation of 1,400,000 copies. The times, of course, were bad. Trade was stagnant and unemployment disastrously and menacingly high. It was the era of Jarrow and the hunger marches. All the same there was reason to believe that, given its share of good fortune, the *News Chronicle* would turn out to be a substantial profit earner.

Efforts to sell *Lloyd's Sunday News* (by now calling itself the *Sunday News*) had been going on for some time, but nobody wanted it, not even it was said for the peppercorn price of

£20,000. Eventually in the year after the *News Chronicle* merger it was disposed of to Lord Camrose and packed into his *Sunday Graphic*. What money changed hands does not appear; it could only have been a modest amount.

At its demise Edgar Wallace was the editor of the *Sunday News*. He was never one to worry about being in attendance at press time and on the Saturday night when its death was announced he was busy producing a new play at Wyndham's Theatre. He knew nothing about what was going on until somebody told him he wasn't an editor any longer because his paper had foundered.

But for all newspaper proprietors who had interests outside London, as United had in Provincial, another worrying factor had to be taken into account: a newspaper Nero was flaunting his purple. Lord Rothermere, at the head of the great *Daily Mail* organisation, had launched his grandiose scheme for a chain of new papers—*Evening Worlds*—in various big centres of population.

Whether he was inspired by envy of the strong hold which Lord Camrose had established in different parts of the country with Allied Newspapers Ltd., or whether it was megalomania alone is now a matter of small, if any, account. The *Catholic News* did not hesitate to say what many were thinking, that Lord Rothermere was acting 'in a manner which it is difficult to reconcile with ordinary sanity.' Rarely did father and son display so remarkable a contrast as the first Rothermere and his sagacious and modest successor, the present viscount. The bombast with which he announced his new Northcliffe Newspapers—so named after his famous brother—takes one's breath away.

Neither he nor his advisers appear to have had the dimmest notion that with every arrogant pronouncement they were offending the local pride and susceptibility of the very people among whom they expected their *Evening Worlds* to sell. *They* were going to show the woaded provincials what a real newspaper should be. *They* were going to give them a genuine metropolitan-brand journal in place of the local product which they had had to suffer for so long.

In Newcastle an *Evening World* had got under way actually with considerable success—'triumphantly' cried the *Daily Mail*, banging all its gongs—but in the event it turned out that the Geordies were more curious than converted and the indigenous *Newcastle Chronicle* gave it a thorough drubbing. (The *Chronicle* was edited at that time with notable skill and native canniness by William Redpath, who was later to become London Editor of Provincial Newspapers.) Another *Evening World* had begun publication at Bristol, and on April 25 1930 came the announcement that Lord Rothermere was going to sweep the board with *Evening Worlds* at Cardiff, Middlesbrough, Sheffield, Hull and Birmingham, and that plans were under consideration for Edinburgh, Preston, Liverpool, Leeds and Belfast. Thus the *Daily Mail* gave due warning of imminent obliteration to Lord Camrose at Cardiff and Sir Charles Starmer at Birmingham, while

> At Hull (it said) Northcliffe Newspapers enter a territory higherto monopolised by Provincial Newspapers Ltd., a company which may be described as the Lloyd's Bank chain of evening newspapers.

The gibe, of course, was aimed at the fact that United and Provincial were leaning heavily on their bankers: and maybe this is the place to put on record that throughout the history of the two companies Lloyd's Bank has rendered them faithful service and collaboration—and in consequence has reaped a just reward for the confidence it was showing at the time when the *Daily Mail* was going off its head. But it was not a *Daily Mail* sneer so much as hard commercial strategy that dictated Provincial's next step.

By now Mr Binder had resigned from the chairmanship of United and Provincial; it had never been intended that he should continue beyond the acute crisis period during which his financial acumen had played so vital a part. He was later to rejoin both boards as a director, but in 1930 Mr Brent Grotrian assumed the two chairmanships—choosing the nominal fee of £100 a year—and the Provincial directorate was reduced to five, the other members being Mr Akerman (managing director), Sir Harry Brittain, Mr T. H. Graham and Mr J. H. Parham.

Brent Grotrian knew a mighty lot more than Lord Rothermere about Hull and its people—after all, he had coped with many an election meeting beside the fish docks—and no doubt the *Hull Daily Mail* could have withstood any assault from an *Evening*

World, but was this the time for Provincial Newspapers to take on the Harmsworth millions in a Humberside battle, with the prospect of hostilities extending to Edinburgh, where it owned the *Edinburgh Evening News,* and Preston, where it was responsible for the *Lancashire Daily Post?*

An adroit compromise was effected, the indefatigable Bernhard Binder acting as Provincial's negotiator. On condition that he kept out of all other territories where Provincial Newspapers functioned, Lord Rothermere was sold the controlling interest in the *Hull Daily Mail* and its associated publications. Provincial retained a 49 per cent. interest, and that 49 per cent. was to play an important part in the successful expansion of the group many years later.

As it fell out Rothermere soon decided that it was useless trying to foist *Evening Worlds* on a public that didn't want them, and Northcliffe Newspapers Ltd. was ultimately built on a process of acquiring existing properties. Today it is an important and prosperous organisation, living in peaceful co-existence with United.

In the annual report of United for 1930 it was disclosed that operations during the year had resulted in a loss of £161,000. To this other sums had to be added, making a total of £223,435. These were the wintry figures that had compelled the *News Chronicle* merger. The new chairman began his address to the annual meeting by apologising for such an unsatisfactory report, but he stressed the trading prospects of the *News Chronicle* and emphasised that the holding in Provincial Newspapers 'should also be of considerable value.' Provincial had earned £181,000 in profits that year.

'After deducting from this figure interest on bank loans and the first preference dividend the proportion of the surplus profits applicable to your company's holding of second preference and ordinary shares would amount to about £63,000. The directors of Provincial Newspapers Ltd. decided however to conserve its resources and to pay no dividend on the second preference and ordinary shares. I do not think that anyone will question the wisdom of this course in the circumstances', said Mr Brent Grotrian.

Such, then, was the position at the end of 1930, and prevailing policy was defined in the chairman's phrase about conserving resources. During the 'thirties Stanley Baldwin produced a word which he was never tired of repeating: 'stability.' That was what United Newspapers was after. But 'stability' does not make news: however necessary it may be at times it represents a dull condition, and the immediately following years in United's history were not exactly sensational. Anyway, there had been enough of sensation.

Occurrences were in line with routine and the few 'alarums and excursions' were commonplace. One episode was the discrete merging of the Northampton *Daily Echo* into Provincial's *Northampton Daily Chronicle* which started an illogical rumour to the effect that Provincial Newspapers as a whole was for sale. *World's Press News* however was 'able to state on the authority of Mr Ivor Griffiths (the then London Editor) that this rumour is entirely without foundation.'

Mr Griffiths painted a rosy picture of Provincial's various papers but he was a little over-enthusiastic when he declared that the *Yorkshire Evening News* was 'going strong.' Maybe it *was* going strong so far as the expenditure of energy was concerned, but not in the way of profitability. In fact it was engaged in what had become a lifetime of gallant but hopeless struggle with the dominant Leeds evening, the *Yorkshire Evening Post*. The two rivals were to battle on for another twenty years, exchanging lively blows in a manner which, in these different days, it is refreshing to recall. At least their conflict made for efficient journalism—journalism with a cutting-edge—and as a result the public of Leeds and the West Riding were well served.

Other papers in the group made money sedately if not excitingly. Provincial's trading profits for the next five years were:

1931	£157,364
1932	£171,572
1933	£177,837
1934	£180,994
1935	£177,642

A picture of 'stability' in action, if such a thing be possible. And what of United, the holding company? It remained quiescently watchful, pursuing a steady course through the difficult 'thirties. Nevertheless this was not a state of affairs that could satisfy the restless spirit of Jack Akerman indefinitely. He paid close attention to the operations of the *News Chronicle* and to the nursing of Provincial but it irked him to feel constrained in 'the fell clutch of circumstance'. He and the chairman (now Sir Herbert Brent Grotrian, Bt., K.C.) met frequently in the desolate old *Daily Chronicle* building where he had his office. At last came a dramatic bid for independence from melancholy entail. It was embodied in this statement issued at the beginning of November 1936:

> Negotiations have been completed for the acquisition by the Daily News Ltd. of the interests of United Newspapers Ltd. and of Westminster Press Ltd. in the *News Chronicle*. By these purchases the Daily News Ltd. will become the sole owner of the share capital of that newspaper.
>
> The purchase price is based on a valuation of the copyright of the *News Chronicle* at approximately £1,000,000.

Clearly Mr Cadbury and Lord Cowdray must have been involved in the discussions that led to this deal, but the impulse came from United. In parting with its share in the *News Chronicle* it received £500,000 in cash and was additionally repaid £100,000 of working capital.

The announcement created much comment, particularly when the implications were studied. Some time later the periodical *Cavalcade*, in its 'Business and Finance' feature, expressed what was the general verdict. It pointed out that by the transaction

> the whole of United Newspapers £502,000 debt had been wiped out and the debt of Provincial Newspapers Ltd. had been reduced from £800,000 to £240,000. This is the story of United Newspapers Ltd., which once made a profit of £300,000 a year and later had floundered in debt and destruction. It is one of the greatest stories of salvage that Fleet Street has known. At one period the $7\frac{1}{2}$ per cent cumulative preference shares were sold at 1s. 6d.—today they are over 25s.

The phoenix had shaken itself free of the ashes and at last was winging its way towards where an open sky seemed invitingly to shine.

Sir William Barnetson. Appointed Chairman 1966

Mr H. C. Drayton. Chairman 1948-1966

3

HITLER INTERVENES

SALISBURY SQUARE has had its face lifted on many occasions. Even in a contemporary lifetime its buildings have been knocked down and re-erected to an extent that has transformed its appearance. Today smooth concrete cubes rise coldly where yesterday the square was surrounded by Edwardian facades of warm brick and ornate pediment, guarded by iron railings.

The home of *Lloyd's Sunday News* and the *Daily Chronicle* was in Salisbury Square and provided United Newspapers with its headquarters during the first two decades of its existence. Then, just before the second World War, came a removal. United and Provincial went into new premises at Number 2. That building has now gone down 'time's ever-rolling stream' in order to make room for something more modern, but it was distinctly modern in its era. If it did not glitter with so much glass, it was reminiscent of the *Daily Express* block in near-by Fleet Street—but only as a thin slice, for unlike the Beaverbrook mansion it was all up-and-down and had no corpulence.

Recent excavations do not appear to have been accompanied by the sensational, but in 1903, when *Lloyd's Sunday News* was laying foundations for new presses, men digging up part of Salisbury Square came upon objects which were found worthy of prompt transference to the British Museum. They included bones of the woolly rhinoceros, the mammoth, the reindeer and 'the great extinct ox (*bos primigenius*)'.

Describing this phenomenon a journalist wrote, 'It is strange, almost beyond the power of words to express, that on the actual area now occupied by some of *Lloyd's* mammoth printing machinery the savage life of prehistoric days roamed through primeval forests'. There are cynics who might see in this a similitude rather than a contrast, deeming that Fleet Street has never wholly discarded the aboriginal discourtesies of the Pleistocene age, but in the business of removing to Number 2 Salisbury Square it is improbable that the staff of United gave a thought to poor *bos primigenius* who had lain for so many millenia in the mud below them.

To the new building went the personnel and apparatus necessary for the London activities of Provincial Newspapers. Here was the metropolitan end of the private wire to Edinburgh, Leeds, Preston, with rediffusion to other centres. Here worked the London Editor with his staff of four or five, Mr Richardson the advertising director, Mr Snelson and his accountants, and of course the managing director, Jack Akerman, together with his chief executive, 'Joe' Parham, a man cut on more broad-shouldered lines than the building. Solid, diligent, experienced, Mr Parham's contribution to the 'stabilisation' of Provincial deserves to be remembered gratefully. He had started his career with the Lloyd paper company and had later been circulation manager of the *Daily Chronicle*. In due course he was to succeed Akerman as managing director.

Within a year or two came the Hitler war, calling a halt to normal commercial enterprise. For the journalists it provided plenty of material, although newsprint rationing brought their papers down to four pages, but managements had to concentrate on problems of communication, distribution, shortages, and various Government controls rather than on development.

Provincial were fortunate in that the towns where their newspapers were located did not come under heavy German bombardment. Edinburgh was but slightly affected. Leeds met with only one visitation from the Luftwaffe, which was described at the time as a 'quarter blitz', and it never had to endure the cruel devastation and heavy loss of life that fell on other Yorkshire cities like Hull and Sheffield. In London 2 Salisbury Square, though often shaken and once deprived of its windows, continued to hold its slim proportions upright.

War may considerably govern but it does not stifle the normal

United Newspapers' old office at Salisbury Square, London, after a landmine blast had sucked the glass out of the windows

vicissitudes of individual life; men came and went in the affairs
of United and Provincial.

In 1941 died one of the rarest characters, Walter M'Phail, who
had edited the *Edinburgh Evening News* for over twenty years and
had been on its editorial staff for more than half a century. His
exact age does not appear to have been known even to his own
paper, but it *was* known that he had started in journalism as far
back as 1881. He was born under the shadow of Edinburgh
Castle, the son of a sergeant in the Highland Light Infantry, and
throughout his life he devoted himself to the welfare and enlightenment of the Scottish capital. He loved every inch of its stone.

Stalwart, stocky, totally unconforming, he strode about the
wynds of Edinburgh in heavy Army boots. He was *persona grata*
to rich and poor alike. If he entered the Court of Session the
presiding judge would incline his head and say quietly, 'Good
morning, Mr M'Phail'—something it is difficult to imagine
happening in the Strand.

As moulded by M'Phail the *Edinburgh Evening News* was a fine
newspaper, responsible, well-written, vigilant. It did not need
to indulge in typographical gymnastics in order to cover a
paucity of thought. Edinburgh trusted it and in consequence it
made a lot of money.

Its sister paper at Leeds, which did not make a lot of money,
nevertheless brought into the organisation another remarkable,
if vastly different character—so different, indeed, that Walter
M'Phail viewed him with much reservation. This was Vladimir
Poliakoff. If he deserves his little niche here it is simply on
account of his shrewdness, his *panache* and his galvanism. 'Polly'
as his English friends called him, was a refugee from the Bol-
shevik revolution. At some period around 1920 he reached
Scotland. He turned his considerable talents to journalism, later
becoming diplomatic correspondent of the *Evening Standard*.
During the Spanish civil war he had an ear to the sounding board
of the Italian dictator and provided the *Evening Standard* with a
number of scoops.

But 'Polly' knew his Fascists and Nazis and had them taped
for what they were. At the approach of the Hitler war the then
editor of the *Yorkshire Evening News*, who had known 'Polly' on
the *Evening Standard*, persuaded him to join Provincial's London

Walter M'Phail, for over twenty years editor of the *Edinburgh Evening News*

team. Under the pseudonym 'Augur' he gave the *Yorkshire Evening News* and its companion papers a series of weekly articles extraordinarily accurate in their judgment and prophecy. They helped the Leeds paper to punch painful dents in the armour of its rival, the *Yorkshire Evening Post*.

Poliakoff was a genuine original. He was often to be seen striding fiercely up Fleet Street, wearing a beret and leading a couple of shaggy Afghan hounds at the end of a clattering chain. He called them Rab and Rib, after Rabinovitch and Ribbentrop. In appearance he could—when required—look as menacing as Il Duce himself, but he was in fact tender-hearted and gracious. Nor were the world's affairs his only interest. He could talk long and fascinatingly about Russian literature and the genius of Turgeniev.

Each paper in the group had its own tale to tell of how Hitler stimulated peculiar activities or encouraged imaginative adaptations. Invasion was expected more than once, especially after Dunkirk, and newspaper editors and managers had their instructions for action should the Germans arrive in their area. The most imperative of these was that all printing machinery should be rendered useless so that the enemy would not be able to publish misleading 'news'. Crowbars, sledge hammers and more subtle secret weapons were disposed at strategic points. A holocaust which, in terms of invested capital, it is horrifying to think about, would undoubtedly have taken place had the necessity arisen.

In at least one office the staff felt that more was demanded than such purely defensive measures. 'Attack! Attack!'—was not that the historic dictum? An old metal pot was reconditioned, ready for emplacement on the top floor overlooking the main entrance in the street below. The idea was that, should German paratroops attempt to enter the building, a stream of molten metal could be ladelled down on them. Medieval, perhaps, but potent. Additionally, a supply of the ingots used in linotype machines was available for similar gravitational discharge. What Nazi would have welcomed one of these on his cranium, dropped from a height of fifty feet?

While the various provincial centres coped with their daily wartime problems the London office carried on, like the rest of London, beneath bombs and rockets. The little editorial staff provided a flow of 'inside information' about the war. Sometimes they sailed close-hauled to the wind and Admiral Thomson, the Press Censor, is known to have had a very high regard for the ingenuity and temerity of 2 Salisbury Square. Redpath, Poliakoff and Denham—he was the 'scientific' expert, learned concerning things like depth-charges and radar—contributed most of this material.

The directorial oversight of Leeds and its requirements was in the hands of a new member of the board, E. J. L. W. Gilchrist, M.C., D.F.C., and the Lancashire papers were the concern of Joe Parham. The two were joint managers of Provincial. Gilchrist had served gallantly with the Royal Flying Corps in the first World War and had sustained severe head wounds. In consequence he was unstable. Sometimes he would display a flash of uncanny perception; sometimes he tried his colleagues grievously with bewildering ideas. His was an unhappy story but the cause of it needs to be respected; and in fact he did a lot to encourage and reinforce the *Yorkshire Evening News* in its battle with the *Yorkshire Evening Post*.

Meantime one who was to play a highly important part in the company's destiny had responded to Akerman's invitation and come along to help him. This was Mr F. R. Lewis. He joined the group in 1940 and in the years to come was managing director of United Newspapers, Provincial Newspapers and the Argus Press.

'Reg' Lewis had served as an infantryman in the first World War and was badly wounded. He was then seconded to the Merchant Shipbuilding Department of the Admiralty and followed Akerman as Controller of Steel. In 1924 he was manager of the dazzlingly successful amusement park at the great British Empire Exhibition at Wembley, later organising exhibitions at Olympia, the Albert Hall and the White City. But his monument in that field is Earls Court, home of the Motor Show and other enterprises.

Reg Lewis built Earls Court as we know it. In 1935 he secured the offer of a long lease on the then building from the Underground railway company, arranged two million pounds-worth of finance, planned and completed the present building, and floated the operating company of which he became managing director. At the same time he continued his various exhibition activities and was instrumental in reviving the National Sporting Club. During the quarter century in which he was so largely responsible for United and Provincial, Mr Lewis retained his seat on the board of Earls Court, retiring from the chairmanship when he became President of the company in 1968.

It would be impossible to assess all he did for United and Provincial or to exaggerate the importance of his contribution right up to the day of his death. Through years of change and the comings and goings not only of individuals but of policies he remained steadfast at the heart of it all, ensuring that the ship was always safely and adroitly trimmed. His quietly-spoken words were always to the point, his mind dead on target. Nobody could pull the wool across Reg Lewis's eyes and he would have been a brave machine-room overseer or linotype mechanic who tried. He acquired an immense knowledge of our complicated industry in all its parts.

At conferences or board meetings Lewis had a way of spotting flaws in arguments, or noting significances which others overlooked, that was quite extraordinary. He was never verbose; he preferred thinking to speaking, and that was his strength. Moreover, he was unassuming and invariably kind, a man not only to admire but for whom one developed affection.

He was appointed to the boards of United and Provincial in 1944, working in close association with Akerman. One evening in the winter of 1946 he was about to clear his desk after the day's problems when Akerman rang him.

'How long will it take you to get home?' asked Akerman.

'An hour.'

'Can you be back at the Hyde Park Hotel in a black tie by 7 p.m. with your wife?'

'I should think so.'

'Right.'

Lewis had no idea what it was all about, but the evening was to prove a turning point in the life of United Newspapers Ltd.

HARLEY DRAYTON

WHEN Mr and Mrs Lewis arrived at the Hyde Park Hotel they discovered that they were to dine with eight others—Sir Herbert and Lady Brent Grotrian, Mr and Mrs Akerman, Mr John Morris (of Rhys Roberts, the company's solicitors) and Mrs Morris—and Mr and Mrs Harold Charles Drayton.

Conversation across the table was of a purely social kind, 'featuring', as the newspapers say, Akerman's humour, Brent Grotrian's dry rejoinders, and Drayton's reminiscence. Not a word was said about business, and indeed to some of those present, particularly the ladies, the reason for it all was no more apparent than the chlorine in the salt of the cruet. Nevertheless business had brought about that dinner party. It was Drayton's way of ascertaining whether he and the characters at the head of United might 'live together' harmoniously.

A few weeks earlier, in conversation with one of the hierarchs of Lloyd's Bank, reference had been made to the property owned by United Newspapers—property of great potential value in the heart of important provincial towns and cities. Drayton had pricked up his ears and his pervasive inquiries had ratified enough to provide a keener interest in the company and its subsidiary.

Some 1,500,000 shares in United, representing the holding of the Inveresk Paper Co. were available for negotiation, and not long after the dinner party at the Hyde Park—the representatives of United having presumably demonstrated their 'liveability'—this large block, equal to about one third of the equity, was bought by the Drayton interests, known to the City as '117 Old Broad Street.'

The deal had not gone through without demur. Drayton jibbed at the price proposed and might have called it off had it not been for one of his trusted collaborators, Mr P. L. Fleming (now on the United board) who, having carefully investigated United, told him bluntly that his hesitations were ridiculous.

At 117 Old Broad Street, Harley Drayton—the name by which he was everywhere identified—had concentrated the direction of his financial empire. It consisted of a number of well-known investment trusts and companies with vast capital assets, of which perhaps British Electric Traction was the principal. Drayton himself had been largely responsible for the immense development of B.E.T. with which he had been associated for many years. At its peak B.E.T. owned more than 14,000 tramcars and omnibuses in this country and overseas, notably Canada, Africa and the West Indies.

Sooner or later Harley Drayton became chairman of most of the other '117 Old Broad Street' concerns. He presided over Antofagasta and Bolivia Railways, the British Lion Film Corporation, the Electrical and Industrial Investment Co., the English and International Trust and Argus Press. He had considerable banking interests and was on the boards of the Midland Bank, the Midland Bank Executor and Trustee Co., and the Philip Hill Investment Trust. He was a member of the council of the Institute of Bankers.

In the City Drayton was celebrated for his uncanny shrewdness in perceiving opportunities for the expansion of little-known undertakings and for a number of dramatic deals. Among these his sale of the Argentine Railways for £150 millions was outstanding. Before his death in 1966 he had extended his activities to television—Associated Rediffusion—and it was alliteratively said of him by *The Times* that his interests ranged from 'nitrates to newspapers, finance and films, banking and building.'

This, then, was the commanding figure who took the helm of United and Provincial in 1947. It was a new field for him and presently he was to count it as the most fascinating into which he had entered. Money and buses and nitrates and railways may tax a man's commercial and fiscal skills; newspapers have a habit of evoking his warmer personal qualities and revealing himself to himself in human terms. This is what Harley Drayton came to enjoy in United.

Yet there was another, and little known, reason why his possession of newspapers gave him satisfaction. The editors who addressed great numbers of people up and down the country were *his* editors, influencing opinion and commenting on affairs. He never interfered with them, they said what they thought with perfect independence, but he was in charge of their organisation. The newspapers were *his* newspapers. He had thus many mouthpieces and his pleasure in this circumstance derived considerably from the fact that during his early years in the City he had often —rightly or wrongly—felt himself snubbed by some who operated there within the tradition of public school exclusiveness.

He never failed cordially to acknowledge the debt he owed to men like Lord St Davids and Mr J. S. Austen, who had recognised his financial genius in youth, but he remembered also that there were others who had looked with disdain on the ill-educated boy from the country who had set himself up in their midst and happened to be just that bit smarter than they were. Everybody came to concede his ability and probity but he could never quite rid himself of this notion. He had no time for false values or stupid vanities. Well—let them read his newspapers!

Harley Drayton was born of humble parents hard by the Lincolnshire village of North Kelsey, near Market Rasen. He himself confessed that he was 'almost uneducated' when, as a lad of fifteen, he answered an advertisement for an office boy in London at a wage of £1 a week. Years afterwards he was chaffed by a colleague who pointed out that *he* had started at ten shillings a week. 'Ah!' flashed Drayton, 'But I'll bet you were living with your parents? Yes? I thought so. *I* had to keep myself in digs with *my* quid a week.'

Nevertheless he was lucky, because it was to the Government Stock and Other Securities Investment Co. that he went as office boy. The head of the company was the Hon. John Wynford Philipps, later Lord St Davids, who quickly spotted his remarkable astuteness and, by increasing his responsibilities, helped him on the road that led to fortune.

When Drayton, with his '117 Old Broad Street' group, took charge of United, he was at the top of his potential and experience, aged 46. He looked the very picture of an English country squire, rubicund, stalwart, with eyes of the brightest blue. Though he usually indulged in the black jacket and striped trousers appropriate to the City, he had a partiality for light grey suiting and in the summertime not infrequently sported a straw boater long after that gear had become archaic. After luncheon he would take a cigar, but his pipe was his more constant companion.

He had a prodigious memory and a mind that was persistently inquisitive. A member of the Provincial board wrote books about early Christianity. He gave Harley Drayton one of them. It was diligently read and for a time was kept in a drawer at 117—presumably for the catechising of City potentates. One day Drayton said to the author: 'You know how Jesus said "Are not two sparrows sold for a farthing"?'

'Yes.'

'Well, he can't have been ignorant of market prices, can he?'

He enjoyed touring the offices where his papers were published. At Leeds, during the period when newsprint was still rationed, he said to Rowland Shawcross, the editor, 'You've got a hell of a big editorial staff.'

'Well, sir', replied Shawcross, 'when you have only four pages to play with—or occasionally six—the job of cutting down and concentrating the news calls for more work than if you have a big paper.'

'H'm.'

About two years later Drayton again visited Leeds. Newsprint was no longer rationed. Again he remarked, 'You've got a hell of a big editorial staff.'

'We have a big paper to fill,' answered the unsuspecting Shawcross. He was promptly reminded that two years earlier he had argued that *small* papers entailed big staffs: did he expect to have it both ways? This is an example of the retentive power of Drayton's mind; it was remarkable when one considers the multifarious demands on his concentration. He enjoyed exercising it but there was no malice in its deployment.

Come August and he would call on his fellow directors to set forth on one of the tours, sometimes to Lancashire, sometimes to Edinburgh, sometimes to Northampton and the Midlands, sometimes to Yorkshire. His quick eye spotted all manner of detail and registered it for reference. An item would crop up at a board meeting in London—say, concerning repairs to some small printing shop on the edge of the Pennines which he had not visited for a few years. He would gaze for a moment at the ceiling and then say, 'Can't we tackle it from that far corner of the yard near the coal-bunker? We could knock down the old brick wall; half the mortar's gone anyway, especially under the coping at the railway end.' How he was able so sharply to re-visualise such a scene when in all probability the Bolivian railway or a South African bank was pressing for an important decision remains a mystery. The financial world always held that he was a bit of an enigma.

The nearer a man was to the soil the quicker Harley Drayton responded to him. Telephones from the City could go on ringing their heads off if he happened to be discussing Landrace pigs with a chap wearing dungy boots somewhere in the Fylde. During his later years he farmed some 700 acres around his beautiful home, Plumton Hall near Bury St Edmunds. Shooting and fishing appealed to him and he was quite an expert ornithologist; but he had a deeper interest which showed that the 'almost uneducated' boy had not been laggardly in catching up. This was book collecting, especially the work of Daniel Defoe. He laid hands on every scrap of Defoe he could find, down to single-sheet pamphlets, and his proudest possession was a first edition of *Robinson Crusoe*. Another passion was for medieval illuminated manuscripts. He bought many of these not always to add to his collection so much as to keep them in their native England.

At home he was a considerate host, a good conversationalist over the claret, but in tackling a business proposition he could be quite brutally rough if he deemed it to be necessary. Plain, even harsh, speech was honourable; he recoiled from smoothness and sophistry.

Harley Drayton did not become chairman of United and Provincial immediately: during 1947 he was content to sit on the boards as an ordinary director until arrangements could be made for him to take over from Sir Herbert Brent Grotrian. At the end of the year Sir Herbert stepped down, having rendered yeoman service. By training he was not a newspaper man and he had relied on Akerman's professional advice, but he never shirked the ultimate responsibility and throughout the dark days he had worked hard and tirelessly to pull the business round, bringing to bear a cool judgment and a steely resolution when things were at their most critical.

It was on January 1 1948 that Drayton formally assumed the chairmanships, and on the selfsame day a young man entered the office of the *Edinburgh Evening News* to start work as a leader writer. His name was William Denholm Barnetson. For United Newspapers it was a unique New Year's Day.

Other changes occurred about this time. Mr Akerman resigned as managing director; he was not in good health. He retained his seat on the boards but Mr Parham succeeded him in the managing directorship. In 1948 Sir Herbert Brent Grotrian retired and his son Mr J. A. B. Grotrian (now Sir John Grotrian, the second baronet) became a director. He has remained on the boards throughout the intervening years and it is a source of pleasure to his colleagues that a name so intimately linked with the evolution of the group should still appear in the list of directors.

Provincial was earning good money. The gross profit for 1947 was £444,411 and for the following year £557,990. Small acquisitions were also made. Nuneaton Newspapers Ltd. was bought in 1947 and remained for many years a part of the organisation before being sold to a Midland company. During 1949 and 1950 Provincial became owners of Country and Sporting Publications Ltd., publishers of *World Sports*—now *Sportsworld*—and other periodicals. Various tidying up operations were completed, like the rearrangement of the greetings card department at Preston.

Jack Akerman did not live long to enjoy his less arduous days. Late in 1950 he died, to the sorrow of all who had cherished his companionship. By that time the joint board had been reduced to seven. Gilchrist had gone and had been replaced by Mr J. R. Grey, but when the Chairman looked round at his fellow-members it can only have been in a meditative mood that he drew on his pipe. Three of the six could hardly have been described as up-and-coming go-getters. Sir Harry Brittain was aged 77. Joe Parham was 76, and Bernhard Binder was 74. 'Time and

34

motion' must have been uppermost in Drayton's reflections, yet he was content for the present to let things bide.

Parham and Reg Lewis knew the ropes and the period was not favourable to bold venture. The whole country was occupied with problems resulting from the war. Readjustment and re-cuperation were prime considerations. A long lag had to be made up. It was no use pushing the boat out flamboyantly into a sea yet treacherous with turbulent tides.

Meantime in Scotland 'Bill' Barnetson diligently discovered and pursued the cunning art of writing leading articles for the *Edinburgh Evening News*. That was not a paper content to fill its editorial column with 'wool.' There had to be a touch of granite in its thought, and James Seager, who had succeeded the doughty M'Phail, was an editor of the same school. He knew his craft and demanded quality work.

As might be expected, Barnetson did not spare himself. Although every evening paper man has to be at his desk early in the day he was often the earliest, and it came to pass that one morning, when he found himself alone in the editorial room, a stocky pink-cheeked Englishman wandered in.

'Good morning', said Barnetson.

'Who are you?' inquired the visitor.

'Oh, I write the leaders. My name's Barnetson.'

'Mine's Drayton.'

Quickly grasping the situation, that Drayton must have arrived on the night sleeper from Kings Cross, Barnetson asked, 'Would you like a cup of tea?' and his first personal service to his boss was to put the kettle on. They chatted about this and that, and in the light of later events it must be assumed that Drayton's perspicacity exercised itself across the office tea-mugs. Perhaps it is infelicitous to say that in this manner the early bird caught the worm—but the moral holds.

In 1954 Joe Parham retired and Mr Lewis became managing director of United. The time was approaching for a reorganisation of the board; it was felt that more professional know-how was needed at the top. Sir Bernhard Binder developed serious eye trouble which ultimately led to total blindness, and his days of service were numbered by age and this cruel affliction.

Mr Barnetson had succeeded James Seager as editor of the

Edinburgh Evening News some years earlier; he had also been given the responsibility of management there. His great ability had been demonstrated in the paper's bounding prosperity, and at the end of 1958 he was elected to the board of Provincial along with the company's most widely experienced manager, Mr K. M. Whitworth.

'Ken' Whitworth had come up the hard way after starting a career in advertising and graduating through a weekly paper in Berkshire. Just before the war he moved to the South London group of weekly newspapers (then owned by Provincial) as advertisement manager. A year later he joined the R.A.F. He saw service in Singapore and Ceylon as Flying Officer and Flight Lieutenant and on the fall of Java became a prisoner of war.

For nearly four years he endured the privation which was the lot of those who fell into Japanese hands. He was moved from one camp to another, in Singapore and Malaya. He never talks about those years or displays bitterness; rather he is a man whose ready helpfulness, humour and integrity have won him a host of friends throughout the newspaper industry. After his release in 1945 he spent six months in Australian hospitals before being allowed to return home.

On getting back he was appointed general manager of the South London weeklies but soon afterwards was invited by Mr Parham to move to Salisbury Square as his personal assistant. Two years later he became general manager of Provincial Newspapers Ltd. His broad grasp of the company's business led to his appointment to the boards of several subsidiaries, including that of Hull and Grimsby Newspapers which Provincial shared with Northcliffe Newspapers at that time. Ken Whitworth has a deep knowledge about practical administration in the industry, especially in the spheres of labour relations, printing and advertising. His work with the Joint Industrial Council for the Printing Trades and on the Evening Newspaper Advertising Bureau in particular won him the esteem of his colleagues. In 1963 he was President of the Newspaper Society. Today, though retired, he remains a valued and energetic member of the board of United, having become vice-chairman in 1973.

The election of Barnetson and Whitworth to the directorate in 1958 strengthened the expertise which Harley Drayton required

Sir Herbert Brent Grotrian, Bt. K.C. Chairman 1930-1947

The present Board of United Newspapers Ltd.

Seated l to r: Sir Kenneth Parkinson
K. M. Whitworth (Vice-Chairman)
Sir William Barnetson (Chairman)
E. A. Walker (Secretary)
Sir John Grotrian, Bt.

Standing l to r: D. B. Anderson (General Manager)
J. G. S. Linacre
P. L. Fleming
Wilfred Moeller
Guy Schofield
F. E. Hudson

Mr. D. R. Stevens joined the Board after this photograph had been taken

for development. In 1962 when Reg Lewis retired from executive work and became vice-chairman of the company the question of the managing directorship had to be settled. Ken Whitworth was obviously due for promotion but at 58 he was within seven years of the retirement age and Drayton was determined to have a younger man also lined up. Moreover he knew who he wanted, and he confided in a colleague.

'The chap I want—the chap we need—is Barnetson', he said.

'Yes.'

'But I don't know whether he'll come.'

'What do you mean?'

'He's such a thoroughgoing Scot, and there he sits on top of the *Edinburgh Evening News*. He's a great broadcaster up there; he's known in all the Edinburgh clubs; in fact he's a leading figure in Scotland. Do you think he'll throw up all that in order to come to London?'

It may seem odd that Drayton should have had such a doubt about a young man so clearly destined for big things, but it reflects an aspect of his capacity to assess men in general and 'Bill' Barnetson in particular. He knew there was a sensitivity there, a thoughtful and literate mind which could not be assumed to react on conventional lines.

However, all was well. Barnetson left Edinburgh for Fleet Street, and he and Whitworth were appointed joint managing directors. The period of dramatic growth for the company was at hand.

5

SIR WILLIAM BARNETSON

'IT was only in 1963 that United took its rightful part in the restructuring of the provincial newspaper industry.' Thus wrote the Press Council in a survey of the company published with its 1970 annual report.

The 'rightful part' was taken on the initiative of two men, Harley Drayton the chairman and William Barnetson, joint managing director. In the case of Barnetson it marked the sudden advance of a career that has intrigued onlookers throughout the last ten years. It marked also the beginning of a process by which, in the same short period, United Newspapers Ltd. has more than doubled the size of the capital it employs and has produced a sevenfold increase in profits. Drayton had seen the man he wanted and the man he wanted has justified his discernment to an extent which Drayton himself could hardly have foreseen.

In January 1972 he became deservedly Sir William Barnetson, but to personal friends all over the world he will continue to be known by the happy contraction that has seemed so excellently to fit his affable and ever stimulating character, 'Bill' Barnetson. (If you want to remember both his initials he says, 'W.D.—same as War Department.')

Without seeming to be fulsome it is not easy to write admiringly about one who is still, thank goodness, very much with us. It is even harder when you have been his friend, and enjoyed his confidence, over many years. Yet the coincidence that his knighthood was bestowed at the very moment when the planning of this story had reached this particular chapter demands a pause for at least a few words by way of estimate before going on to recount the events of the last decade.

What lies at the heart of his success in one of the toughest fields of endeavour? It is not just that he is a clever man, which is self-evident, or that he moves with confidence in himself. It is not just an intuitive commercial *nous*, or the capacity to flicker figures at his fingertips. He has a considerable academic background and is, as they say, 'widely read', and a linguist: these are assets not extensively shared by others. His practical experience as writer, editor, and newspaper manager gives him an advantage over less fortunate proprietors. He is gregarious, has travelled the world, knows the people one should know both at home and abroad, and they like him. He can also bide his time.

These things add up to an impressive amalgam; but the rare gift of the gods which fuses them to such effectiveness in the individual Barnetson is a genius for simplification and the sharp focusing of an objective.

No man ever had a more sinewy skill in burrowing to the distant chink of an opportunity—or exposing an illusion—and clearing away obstructions and distractions. His ability to mould a problem to its simplest shape, or reduce a proposition to its simplest outline, is remarkable. One has only to hear him talking about some complex, fogbound affair to realise that his mind has an orderliness to which few attain and his vision a clarity which many must envy. He pushes away non-essentials as a snowplough shifts the snow. But where he differs from men of overweening presumption is that he never pushes aside people. He is sensitive not only to their views but to their personalities and experience. While leading the way he seeks and derives strength from his colleagues and is prepared to modify.

For all his mercantile acumen it is the journalist in him which prevails. He knows that a newspaper, and therefore a newspaper business, prospers within the humanities and that the sciences do not suffice. He deploys an ample imagination which has illumined the path for United in many a venture, and if, when giving this imagination its head, he is apt to ignore other matters to the impatience of subordinates, he can suddenly explode his reflective processes with a tangential swoop into the irrelevant or ludicrous. Then he will put down his pipe, throw up his arms like 'a prophet new inspired', and recite a pawky Scots story in faultless vernacular. It is part of a charm that stems from an appreciation of life's illogicalities—an appreciation realised keenly by so logical and literate a mind.

He is quick to praise, slow to condemn, ready to laugh. These make for leadership that draws a response both warm and eager. The word 'tycoon', in its proper Japanese meaning, typifies a man who operates like an unpredictable shotgun. Sir William Barnetson will never be a tycoon because he is something more significant and discriminating.

Of Scottish parents, he was born in Edinburgh fifty-eight years ago. At Edinburgh University (Master of Arts) he studied classics, law, and international relations. During the Spanish civil war he betook himself to Spain and tried his hand successfully at freelance journalism.

On the outbreak of the Hitler war he joined A.A. Command and when hostilities were ending was seconded for special duty which brought him into the world of newspapers and publishing. His fluent German equipped him admirably for the task, which was that of reorganising the newspaper and book production industry in the British Zone. He was responsible for choosing suitable individuals to be licensed to publish newspapers, books and periodicals in a land that had been under the rigid censorship of Dr Goebbels. One of those he selected was a young man called Axel Springer who at that time had little more than a table and an old typewriter at his disposal. Today he is Europe's most prosperous and powerful publisher, a steadfast friend of Sir William Barnetson.

Completion of the German assignment brought him home to Scotland and, like many another officer, he was without any clearly defined career route and almost 'skint.' He had his academic qualifications which enabled him to take up lecturing, but the tug of journalism was insistent, and he seized the opportunity to join the *Edinburgh Evening News* as leader writer when it came in 1948. The pay was hardly lavish and for many months he worked almost round the clock to supplement it, preparing papers, writing leaders and articles, and every evening after office hours giving classes on current affairs and broadcasting on literary and social subjects.

His activities were such that he gathered a large circle of friends in Scottish official, professional and commercial life, and when, a few years later, he took charge of United's business in Edinburgh he was himself, as Drayton rightly judged, an influential figure in Scottish affairs.

The rest has been told. In 1962 he found himself Drayton's chief of staff at a moment which Drayton deemed the right moment for expansion of the company.

Both men shared a conviction that has guided boardroom discussions ever since the day they put their heads together: expansion of the company was not the same thing as acquisition for its own sake. Given the money, it is comparatively easy to snap up papers here, there and everywhere, but the practice leads to obesity rather than to developing vigour. United had to grow to a logical pattern that would ensure a viable harmony of all its parts. Haphazard gobblings would not secure this end; they might well produce problems more abundantly than profits.

For many weeks the staff at Salisbury Square were intrigued by the 'Barnetson mystery.' They saw him come to the office in the morning and sometimes they saw him leave in the evening, though often he stayed long after they had departed. What was he up to throughout the livelong day? Ken Whitworth, his collaborator in the managing-directorship, dealt with company routines and met the problems of various departments. Was the other half of the top executive just a 'sleeping' partner?

Not sleeping indeed, but very acutely awake. Locked in an office fastness, Barnetson was working out a grand strategy that should govern the operations of United Newspapers for the next decade. The existing base in Lancashire had to be fortified and broadened to stop undermining encroachments from competitors. The prosperous Midlands bade fair to become even more prosperous and Northampton was potentially most valuable. The company's spinal column, though only germinal at this stage, was seen to follow a course from the industrial North to the industrial heart of England—a sort of Pennine way—its vertebrae being evident at Preston, Leeds, Doncaster and Northampton. Edinburgh was the most profitable unit of all, yet it lay distant from the area of natural consolidation and potential growth. Hull, too, where United still had a minority interest, was rather isolated.

Along this Pennine Way it was in Yorkshire that United had

to meet stern and intimate competition. At Preston and North-ampton competition was felt from a distance, but at Leeds and, in a subsidiary degree, at Doncaster there was daily conflict with Yorkshire Post Newspapers, whose *Yorkshire Evening Post*, the mightily prosperous stable companion of their famous morning newspaper, exchanged relentless fire with United's *Yorkshire Evening News*.

Such traditional combatants were these twain, and for so many decades had they assaulted each others' redoubts with never a hint of quarter, that a kind of love-hate relationship had grown up, like that which exists between the County Cricket clubs of Lancashire and Yorkshire. Their war was an exclusive affair; one felt that if anybody else intervened the two would combine to oust the intruder before resuming mutual hostilities.

Dreams that some day events might indeed lead to a combina-tion of forces glimmered intermittently, like peeps of wan sun-shine through the sulphurous smoke of battle; but they were only dreams and faded in the hard face of actuality. Nevertheless dreams *can* come true ...

A small tactical operation heralded United's larger offensive. It was calculated to strengthen the eastern flank of important possessions in Lancashire. The company owning two weekly newspapers, the *Nelson Leader* and the *Colne Times*, was finding things increasingly difficult. This was due in great measure to a factor which burdened many local weeklies—the necessity of having to staff and maintain their printing plants. United bought the company in January 1963 and was able to eliminate this burden by closing down the local printing works and transferring the work and the personnel to its plant at Burnley, only a few miles away. This was an example of the way in which a group can, at one and the same time, safeguard the continuance of local newspapers and consolidate its own regional position.

A more significant transaction occurred in August. One of those 'peeps of wan sunshine' just referred to pierced the Northern battlefield with unaccustomed warmth. A modest deal took place between United Newspapers and Yorkshire Post Newspapers. The Barnetson plan had not envisaged this but it was welcome.

At that time it suited Yorkshire Post Newspapers to rid

themselves of their Doncaster weekly, the *Doncaster Chronicle*, so United bought the goodwill and merged the *Chronicle* in the *Gazette*, and both companies felt there was a modicum of reason in it all. Neither side foresaw that, within three years, the *Doncaster Gazette and Chronicle* would be under their mutual ownership, but such is the way of things when newspapers are on the move.

The time was now at hand when the first important operation conceived in Barnetson's strategy had to be undertaken. Before it was realised there was a clearing of the decks for action.

Considerations due not only to the envisaged expansion but to other matters imposed the necessity of abandoning Salisbury Square as United's headquarters. The slim, tower-like, building was sold for development of the site; very soon the last resting place of poor *bos primigenius* was to be scarified again. On April 12 1963 United moved into the old Argus Press premises at 23-27 Tudor Street. Ampler accommodation for the various departments was thus assured, and internal alterations presently carried out provided a modern entrance hall and other facilities, including a more appropriate boardroom on the first floor.

Opposite United's new G.H.Q., on the other side of Tudor Street (just eastward of a notable hostelry, the White Swan, or more familiarly the Mucky Duck) stood Northcliffe House, home of the *Daily Mail*, and it was in that direction—the direction of Viscount Rothermere's Associated Newspapers Ltd.—that United now advanced.

It will be recalled that way back in the 1920s the hard-pressed Provincial Newspapers had sold 51 per cent. of the equity of the *Hull Daily Mail* to the first Lord Rothermere in order to stave off an assault from Northcliffe Newspapers. Now United wanted cash to further its aims, and the Barnetson plan rested considerably on getting this cash in return for the remaining 49 per cent. interest in the Hull concern.

In October 1963 Harley Drayton had a talk with Lord Rothermere, and the deal went through expeditiously and cordially. Rothermere bought United's 49 per cent. for £1,700,000 in cash —a handsome lump sum for the kitty.

Dividends from the *Hull Daily Mail* had been a valuable source of revenue for United; now, of course, they ceased, and no time had to be lost in making the next move. It was provided for in the Barnetson plan, though not in precise terms, for it depended on clarifying, to United's advantage, the persistent murmurings of Roy Thomson (now Lord Thomson of Fleet). He had been bothered for a long time by the position in Edinburgh where he owned the *Edinburgh Evening Dispatch* which had been pounded to impotence by United's thriving *Edinburgh Evening News*. The *Dispatch* had become a millstone round Thomson's neck and he wanted to do a deal that would enable him to cast it off. Approaches had been made to Drayton via Henry Grunfeld of Warburgs, but Drayton resolutely refused to have anything to do with them. He knew when prevarication paid.

By this time Mr Barnetson was a director of the Press Association. One murky autumn day, after a board meeting, he was walking up Fleet Street with a P.A. colleague, Mr Angus Burnett-Stuart of the Thomson Organisation. Suddenly a deluge descended from the lowering clouds and they took shelter in a shop doorway, where an interesting conversation developed.

Burnett-Stuart told Barnetson that Thomson had firmly made up his mind to make a bid for United Newspapers, lock, stock and barrel; and in terms which "neither the United board nor the shareholders could possibly turn down." At that time, the losses on the *Yorkshire Evening News* were heavier than ever; the profits of the group as a whole were nothing to write home about; and United were in no condition to fight off the kind of bid that might be expected. What was to be done?

This apparent bombshell failed to pulverise Barnetson's nervous system. He realised, of course, that Roy was going after the United group simply to acquire the *Edinburgh Evening News*. Against that background, and with the rain still splashing around their feet, he and Burnett-Stuart discussed less draconian —and, from United's point of view, less disagreeable—alternatives, including a possible swop.

Barnetson became tentative, fanciful, exploratory. 'I wonder', said he, 'what about Sheffield?' Thomson's Sheffield newspapers would suit United admirably, not only for their intrinsic value but because they sat close to the *Yorkshire Post* domain and the distant dream. Such a consideration, such a dream, was, of course, not immediately apparent to Burnett-Stuart, and this unexpected suggestion rather intrigued him.

'Well now, that *might* be on.'

'I tell you what', said Barnetson, 'you tackle Roy and go through the motions of making a swop, and get him to invite Harley to lunch.'

'Very well.'

Barnetson lost no time in hurrying to Drayton's London home in Kensington Palace Gardens and briefing him on the situation. A few days later Thomson and Drayton lunched together, Burnett-Stuart having been at work on Roy. The coffee was accompanied by Thomson's thrustful question.

'What about a swop?'

'What do you mean?' parried Drayton, seemingly all innocence.

'What about my Sheffield for your Edinburgh?'

A moment's pause, and then, 'Suits me', said Drayton.

Which only goes to show that spadework even, if necessary, in inclement weather, remains the classic preliminary to a lucrative crop.

The transaction thus swiftly agreed was formally completed in November 1963. United Newspapers exchanged the *Edinburgh Evening News* for the *Sheffield Telegraph* and the Sheffield evening *Star* and made a balancing payment in cash of £564,700. The Pennine Way was immediately strengthened, though there was much regret at having to part with that fine newspaper in Edinburgh.

Things were now moving apace and they were also moving on another initiative which fitted-in perfectly. At Leeds the Yorkshire Post board had become more and more exasperated by the continuing presence of United's *Yorkshire Evening News*, a presence that imposed competitive expenditure on their *Yorkshire Evening Post*. The *Evening Post* was by far the stronger of the two and they knew that the *Evening News* was losing money. Would it not make sense if Harley Drayton could be persuaded to sell them the *News* so that they could close it down and leave the *Evening Post* with a clear field?

Mr Colin Forbes Adam, chairman of Yorkshire Post Newspapers, and his vice-chairman, the late Lord Ingleby, made an appointment to see Drayton at 117 Old Broad Street. When they arrived Barnetson also was present. Appropriate courtesies soon developed into tough talk on both sides, in the midst of which Drayton suddenly sprang a mine.

'What are we talking about?' said he. 'We don't need to sell the *Yorkshire Evening News* at all; we've just made a Sheffield deal with Roy Thomson.'

This was dramatic news for the visitors from the North because at that time the Sheffield operation had not been made public. It changed the position and thickened the atmosphere still further. Forbes Adam and Ingleby left 117 to discuss matters anew with their financial advisers.

They had been suggesting a cash payment which Drayton had resisted but now, after further deliberation, they proposed purchasing the goodwill and copyright of the *Yorkshire Evening News* in return for the issue of 130,000 £1 ordinary shares in Yorkshire Post Newspapers—some 20 per cent. of the equity.

United agreed promptly but on the other side the proposal had to be authorised at an Extraordinary General Meeting of Yorkshire Post shareholders. This took place in December at the office in Albion Street, Leeds, and Barnetson attended. It had been agreed that, should the deal be approved, the *Yorkshire Evening News* would announce the fact and its own immediate demise. But what if the shareholders should refuse their consent? The outcome could not be assumed.

Barnetson devised what seemed to be an adroit plan. An emissary from the *Evening News* was to wait in the yard beneath the room where the meeting was in progress. If the vote was favourable Barnetson would open a window overlooking the yard and give a prearranged signal, upon which the emissary would run the couple of hundred yards to the *Yorkshire Evening News* office in Trinity Street, carrying with him the news of his paper's death.

The shareholders did indeed approve the deal and Barnetson rushed to the selected window. Alas! he could not get it open. Coats of paint diligently applied over a century held it in a leaden grip. For a while he struggled with the stubborn frame but in the end he had to career down the stairs and into the yard in order breathlessly to tell the tidings. That night the *Yorkshire Evening News* announced that it had appeared for the last time. A long, well-fought newspaper war was over and the weaker antagonist had at last succumbed.

On neither side was there joy in the fact itself, for newspaper people cannot see a paper disappear without sadness, and Frank Heywood and Jim Mather, the last general managers of the *News*, had fought tenaciously to promote their paper; but both companies were strengthened by the operation and in the result little, if any, hardship was imposed on the Trinity Street staff. Many, from different departments, were taken on by Yorkshire Post Newspapers and compensation was amicably agreed for others.

United still had the money paid by Rothermere for the Hull shares and this now went towards the purchase of a highly prosperous business at Blackpool. The *West Lancashire Evening Gazette*, the weekly *Blackpool Gazette and Herald* and other local weeklies were owned by the Grime family. Rumour had filtered through Lancashire and into Fleet Street that Sir Harold Grime and his brother, Mr Herbert Grime, were toying with the possibility of joining a group. They were by no means convinced yet, conscious of the changing pattern in the industry, they were pondering the future prospects for a family concern. In particular they were anxious lest unfavourable pressures of some unforeseeable nature should militate against the character and journalistic liberty of the papers they had created.

Mr Barnetson passed them a message through Donald Anderson, the general manager of United's *Lancashire Evening Post* at Preston. He would like to meet the Grimes. They said 'Very well', and he went to Blackpool in April 1964. On the appropriate morning it rained prodigiously, as it had done during that shop doorway conversation in Fleet Street. Between the Imperial Hotel and the *Evening Gazette* office Barnetson suffered such a drenching that it was an apparition emitting steam which confronted Herbert and Harold Grime when he arrived.

He had to answer many probing questions from the two brothers. They wanted to know just what sort of people they were talking to. How did United conceive its responsibilities in owning newspapers? What were its aims and purposes apart from earning money? What of editorial freedom? In what way were they prepared to consider the continuing activity of the Grime family within the business?

Over the next few months further meetings took place. The Grimes were in no hurry; they had no need to be; but as assurances were given and specific details were worked out, they began to like the look of United, and at last they went to London and breakfasted with Mr Drayton and Mr Barnetson at Kensington Palace Gardens. Drayton suggested a figure; Herbert Grime countered with a bigger one. In the end the age-old move was made; they split the difference. The deal was formalised in September 1964 and it has proved to have been a very happy event, leading to cordial personal friendships and mutual prosperity.

As visualised in the general strategy, Lancashire had now become a powerful, integrated base for United, and further operations in 1965 added significant strength and resilience. In March the *Chorley Guardian* was acquired. On the face of it this was not a very consequential proceeding, but it was realised that Chorley would be at the heart of the enormous industrial development area planned for central Lancashire.

Hearing that the board of the *Chorley Guardian* had pondered an approach from elsewhere, Barnetson promptly invited them to meet him. They agreed. 'But not in Chorley', they said, 'lest rumour should get around.' They actually met at one of Mr Forte's establishments on the Lancashire motorway where preliminary polite conversation took place seated on benches, eating pie and chips.

Presently the company adjourned to what was described as a 'private room.' It turned out to be an apartment poised over the roaring highway, where the fridge was kept. The traffic thundered by, the fridge intermittently uttered those singular noises which only a fridge knows how to make, and every other minute a waitress tripped in to fetch a raspberry sundae or a banana split. Despite these variegated diversions the deal was completed to everybody's satisfaction.

Two months later United acquired that splendid property, the *Wigan Observer*, adding a modern web-offset plant to its many other facilities in Lancashire.

Early in 1966 Harley Drayton apologised for his absence from a board meeting; he had a heavy cold. His malady, however, was much more sinister and soon afterwards he underwent an exploratory operation at the London Clinic.

During his period in hospital Barnetson was a frequent visitor, and on one occasion Drayton asked in conspiratorial tones, 'Bill, do you think you could manage to get me a couple of bottles of claret in here?' He chose the vintage year, saying his butler would identify the wine.

Going down the hospital corridor, Barnetson met the physician in charge of the case. 'Harley's asking for claret', he said, wondering whether it would be wise to let him have it.

'Bring it', replied the doctor, 'and let him think nobody knows', so the claret was duly smuggled in beneath Barnetson's overcoat.

The patient was taken back to Kensington Palace Gardens where Barnetson saw him a day or two before his death. Pulling himself up in bed, he said in his now weak voice, 'Thank you for everything, Bill. Give my love to the boys.'

Harley Drayton died on April 7 1966. It was a day of daffodils, sunshine and snowflakes when he was buried in the country churchyard near his Suffolk home.

6

THE BIG YEAR

BY unanimous vote William Denholm Barnetson was elected Chairman of United Newspapers at a board meeting on April 27 1966. Mr Lewis, the vice-chairman, had previously consulted each member of the board individually, but there was never a doubt in anybody's mind about who should succeed Harley Drayton. No man assumed office sustained by more goodwill and admiration from his colleagues.

Shortly afterwards two newcomers joined the directorate as representative of the 117 Old Broad Street interests. They had both been closely associated with Harley Drayton and were, and are, well-known figures in financial and commercial circles in the City—Mr P. L. Fleming and Mr W. Moeller. Wilfred Moeller took his first steps in chartered accountancy under the wing of Sir Bernhard Binder who had done so much for United in its desperate years. Pat Fleming mingles a masterly knowledge of the City and company practice with a partiality for literature and the classics.

Within a month of these changes, and as if in token of things to come, United Newspapers and Yorkshire Post Newspapers forged their first link, at Doncaster.

For many years when the *Yorkshire Evening Post* and the *Yorkshire Evening News* were fighting one another both papers had published editions at Doncaster. These localised versions were not renowned for their profitability but where one functioned the other had to function. Now that the *Yorkshire Evening News* had died, and there was no need for the remaining Leeds paper to produce a Doncaster edition, the opportunity occurred for a development that had long been meditated by Mr Forbes Adam, the Yorkshire chairman. This was to establish a separate evening newspaper at Doncaster. In May 1966 a new company was formed, Doncaster Newspapers Ltd. Yorkshire Post Newspapers held 51 per cent. of the capital, and in consideration of £89,000 in cash and the transfer of the weekly *Doncaster Gazette*, United Newspapers acquired the other 49 per cent. Mr F. E. Hudson, vice-chairman of Yorkshire Post Newspapers, became chairman of the new company and Mr Barnetson and Mr Whitworth joined its board. Thus for the first time the two concerns found themselves engaged in a mutual enterprise. The first issue of the *Doncaster Evening Post* appeared in September 1966.

Now followed nearly three years of comparative quietude—years in which United consolidated its position. Mr Barnetson, tirelessly aided by Ken Whitworth, tightened up the structure, visiting all the offices and printing centres and making himself even more familiar with the personnel and their problems. Where necessary economies were effected, where expansion looked promising capital was provided for plant and staff. The great rebuilding operation at Sheffield, begun by the Thomson Organisation before United took control, was pressed forward and new machinery installed. All this tidying-up, this disposition of forces and re-gearing, was carried out in preparation for the next general advance. It came in 1969.

That year was to prove historic. During its twelve months the activities of United Newspapers absorbed the attention of Fleet Street and the City. By December the company was not only twice as big as it had been in January but was the possessor of world-famous publications which added immensely to its journalistic stature.

The year began with a comparatively modest transaction. Since 1939 United had owned a number of London suburban weeklies called the South London group, operating mainly in the Surrey outskirts. To these it now added a similar series in north London by acquiring the business of the *Hornsey Journal* and its associated papers. London was not a field which United wanted particularly to exploit, but as an asset these profitable weeklies, half encircling the capital, were very valuable and, as will be seen, the deal was far-sighted. It had hardly been completed before a more effulgent orb swam into Barnetson's ken.

Sometime during the winter of 1968 he was talking on the telephone to a fellow-director in the provinces. The immediate business having been settled, his colleague, sensing some restrained excitement in the chairman's voice, asked as if casually, 'Well, and how are things going generally, Bill?'

There was a pause, and then, 'I can't talk openly to you on the phone; it's too delicate. But does the word *Charivaria* mean anything to you?'

'Yes, it does.'

'Well—something's moving.'

'Say no more. I'm with you.'

The word *Charivaria*, of course, was the word which for years had appeared on the first page of *Punch*, above a medley of entertaining items. In the realm of polysyllables charivari is to topical hubbub what salmagundi is to a culinary mess.

It appeared that *Punch*, if not exactly looking for a new home, was a little fearful of falling into the hands of an insensitive landlord. Its proprietors, Bradbury Agnew and Co., were passing through no easy times. Mr Peter Agnew, the chairman, was increasingly worried about the future of a business in which his family was intimately involved. Takeover was a menace for concerns with considerable capital commitments and only modest profits. Among other possibilities was one that did not appeal. Mr Robert Maxwell, at that time keenly active, might see Bradbury Agnew as an attractive proposition and make the kind of offer it would be difficult to resist.

Mr Barnetson, with a sharp ear to the ground, was aware of this situation. A meeting was arranged with Mr Agnew and other members of his family. It took place at 117 Old Broad Street and quick progress was made; subject to further scrutiny and the views of other directors, it was agreed that United should buy Bradbury Agnew for shares.

The pros and cons were debated at length by the United board when the chairman reported back. It was realised that the proposition meant entering the periodical business, which was something rather different from newspapers. It was further appreciated that great energy and enterprise would be necessary to bring *Punch* into healthy viability. Nevertheless Bradbury Agnew owned important printing establishments, like Pulmans of Bletchley, the Leagrave Press at Luton, and the Saffron Hill, London, works where *Punch* was printed. Additionally it had that admirable quarterly, *The Countryman*, and a series of authoritative farming monthlies. The board approved the transaction which went through in April 1969.

What concerned his colleagues was the amount of additional work thrust on the chairman by the absorption of Bradbury Agnew. He had to exert his journalistic imagination towards sustaining the editorial policy of *Punch* and his business skill in tackling the losses being incurred at Pulmans and Saffron Hill. In the end Saffron Hill was closed down and the printing of *Punch* transferred to Bletchley. There were other problems in abundance and they were only overcome by tenacity and resourcefulness.

This period also imposed responsibilities on Bill Barnetson which were not strictly those of United Newspapers although they brought prestige to the company and honour to himself. A particular mark of esteem was his election to the chairmanship of the Press Association during its centenary year. It involved him in a spate of travelling and speech-making up and down the kingdom, and in the organising of a notable London reception which was graced by the Queen. He was also moving into the chairmanship of Reuters, in due course contributing a new dynamism to that famous institution. Other activities included membership of the Press Council. The tide in his affairs was at its flood throughout 1969 and 1970 and he took it, but it meant hard graft.

Meantime United had been steadily buying Yorkshire Post shares on the market—at increasingly higher cost. Up went the price and up went the eyebrows at Tudor Street when lots became available for purchase; nevertheless the purchases were made and by the summer of 1969 United owned some 35 per cent. of the Yorkshire equity.

On the board of the Press Association was Mr J. G. S. Linacre, managing director of Yorkshire Post Newspapers. After a fine war record with Bomber Command (A.F.C. and D.F.M.) Gordon Linacre was forging for himself an equally distinguished career in the newspaper world. He had editorial as well as managerial experience and had held important appointments

E

with the Thomson Organisation before going to Leeds to take executive charge of the Yorkshire Post business. He and Barnetson had known one another well since the days of the Sheffield 'swop', and one evening they dined together at the Savoy.

During the meal Linacre cast a fly in his most accomplished and delicate style. It was perhaps—just perhaps—not quite beyond the bounds of possibility that some sort of agreement might be reached. Of course there would be many things to explore but both men agreed that the time for exploration had arrived. The upshot was that Barnetson arranged to talk further with Sir Kenneth Parkinson (who had succeeded Mr Forbes Adam as chairman of Yorkshire Post Newspapers) and Linacre.

They had a long session shortly afterwards and on this occasion Wilfred Moeller joined them. Sympathy between Wilfred and Sir Kenneth was immediately established when they realised they were both cricketing enthusiasts. (Sir Kenneth is now President of the Yorkshire County Club.) All four men knew that the tide was flowing towards an association of their businesses and nobody was evasive; important considerations were raised at once. Sir Kenneth was rightly concerned about the maintenance of the character of the *Yorkshire Post* and its traditional political outlook; also about the continuance of the Yorkshire board. These were not stumbling-blocks to Barnetson for United had a lively appreciation of the qualities upon which the Yorkshire business had been built—who could know better? Much progress was made at that first full exchange of views; in fact the ground was cleared for decisive action.

Mr Barnetson reported on the state of affairs to his fellow directors who, after discussion, authorised him to enter into detailed negotiation. A similar debate took place at Leeds and the result of it all was that Barnetson was invited to meet the board of Yorkshire Post Newspapers at the Queens Hotel in Leeds. When he reached the hotel on the appointed day he asked in which room the meeting was being held.

'Number 117, sir.'

Could anything have been more auspicious? Reflecting on all that 117 Old Broad Street had contributed to United's progress, Barnetson stepped into the lift convinced that everything would go well. Nor was he mistaken. He had expected to be grilled—

and turned round on the grill—by a platoon of craggy characters; instead he met a number of courteous gentlemen who had very little to ask of him—except that he should take a drink with them.

Sir Kenneth Parkinson explained the earlier conversations and went over the assurances that had been agreed, assurances which guaranteed the editorial freedom of their papers and the continuance of the Leeds board as appropriately representative of Yorkshire life.[1] And that was that. In the ensuing silence Sir Linton Andrews, the editor of the *Yorkshire Post* for many years, remarked, 'What a marvellous thing it is that a merger like this should have been brought about on the initiative of people with real newspaper knowledge!' Nobody knew better than Sir Linton how some newspapers had been tossed about by financiers, politicians and merchants who could not have written a line of good copy between them.

Taking his cue, Barnetson recalled that some twenty years earlier he had been invited to apply for the job of chief sub-editor of the *Yorkshire Post*—and the occasion passed off with cordiality and laughter over a hospitable meal. Barnetson and Tom Chalton, a Yorkshire Post director, exchanged reminiscences of the war when they had served together. Everybody was happy. Subsequent history has justified the most sanguine expectations.

It was October 1969 when the details were published. United Newspapers acquired the entire equity of Yorkshire Post Newspapers. The total cost, including shares previously bought, was £8,408,564. But the spirit behind the whole affair was not one of vendor and purchaser; rather it was one of men imbued with the same sense of trusteeship taking a practical step to ensure new strength and security for the future of their newspapers in a rapidly altering economy. Symbolic of this was an interchange of directors which immediately took place. Sir Kenneth Parkinson, Mr F. E. Hudson and Mr Linacre of Yorkshire Post Newspapers joined the board of United and Mr Barnetson, Mr Wilfred Moeller and Mr Guy Schofield of United joined the Yorkshire Post board.

---

[1] An example of this occurred in 1973 when the long association of the Beckett family with the *Yorkshire Post* was happily restored by the election of Lord Grimthorpe to the board. At the same time the West Riding textile industry provided another director in Mr P. G. D. Marshall.

Wilfred Moeller had done a lot of the involved detail work inherent in this big operation, and tribute must be paid to another who, in the Yorkshire Post negotiations as in all the rest stimulated by Messrs Drayton and Barnetson, had had to get down to complicated figures and fiduciary finickings of the most exacting character—Mr E. A. Walker, the secretary of United. 'Johnny' Walker has been a popular member of the board since the Drayton era. Like all first-rate accountants he has to carry the burden of a conscience, but even when submerged beneath mountains of mathematics, and when his brow is twisted with the turmoil of mental arithmetic, he somehow manages to look at life humorously and can produce a timely witticism to humanise, if not to explain, the most recondite equation. His opposite number, Basil Clough, secretary of the Yorkshire company, and Brian Muffitt who also had a lot of figure-wading to do, has likewise an eye that can twinkle through dire obfuscation.

Sir Kenneth Parkinson and Mr Hudson brought to the United board minds experienced in business. Sir Kenneth is a prominent figure in the Bradford textile industry while Mr Hudson's commercial interests are in engineering. Both are Yorkshire landowners and sportsmen with family roots deep in the county.

So at the close of 1969 Mr Barnetson could have sat back and contemplated a year of astonishing achievement. He *could* have done so, but the swing of events left him little opportunity. The integration of Bradbury Agnew and the Yorkshire Post was a continuing process. Leeds was engaged on a £5,000,000 rebuilding scheme, the old Yorkshire Post premises being no longer capable of meeting the company's needs. Gordon Linacre shouldered the onerous job of supervising this vast development, ably supported by the indefatigable Peter Barker, general manager and a director of Yorkshire Post Newspapers. Endless diligence and patience it needed day and night, but it was a commitment also requiring steady estimating at Tudor Street now that United had the ultimate responsibility.

When Mr Whitworth retired from the joint managing-directorship on reaching the age of 65 Mr Barnetson chose as his chief executive Mr D. B. Anderson, who was appointed general manager of United. Donald Anderson had distinguished himself by his energy as manager of the *Lancashire Evening Post*, a young man with a lot of experience and inherited newspaper flair—his father had at one time been in charge of the *Yorkshire Evening News*. He came to London and 'played himself in', gradually relieving the chairman of many management affairs. He was heartily welcomed to the board in 1972.

With the year 1970 came the next addition to the group, this time a buttressing of the Yorkshire position. The company concerned was The Reporter Ltd., owners of the weekly *Dewsbury Reporter* and *Batley News*, a well-conducted and prosperous concern in the heart of the industrial West Riding. Negotiations were not easy for by lifelong tradition the business was devoted to the Liberal Party, of which its papers were adamantine pillars. If its directors harboured misgivings about attaching themselves to any group, those misgivings were intensified when the approach came from a group owning the Tory *Yorkshire Post*.

Sir Ronald Walker, the nonagenarian but penetratingly shrewd chairman of The Reporter, called a meeting at his home in Dewsbury. His fellow-directors, ladies and gentlemen of stalwart character, confronted Mr Barnetson. It was not just money they were after; it was another kind of principle as well—Liberal principle.

'The *Dewsbury Reporter* must support the Liberal cause', said Sir Ronald. 'Can't you give us some definite assurance, Mr Barnetson—some idea of your company's convictions and standards—something we can approve?'

'Yes, of course' replied Barnetson. 'It would be an exaggeration to say we are dedicated upholders of the Liberal Party, but I can assure you on two things. Firstly, we are against sin, and secondly, we stand for peace, retrenchment and reform.'

There was a moment's silence in the room; then came just a flicker of a smile on Sir Ronald's venerable features as he pronounced his verdict—'That's good enough.'

At the end of 1970 the burden of expenditure on the Leeds rebuilding operations was relieved by the sale of the South London and Hornsey papers to the Argus Press Ltd. United received £1,050,000 in cash and it was not long before all indebtedness was cleared; the company was enjoying a high earnings flow.

Mr Barnetson received his knighthood in the New Year honours of 1972. The news gave genuine pleasure not only to his

Group editors confer at Harrogate

friends but to Fleet Street and the newspaper world as a whole; but those who have read this story will realise that it came also to crown that decade of grand strategy which had begun in 1962. And it is peculiarly interesting that the last acquisition of the decade was made with the selfsame motive which inspired the first. In 1963 the *Nelson Leader* had been bought in order to fortify the company's flank in eastern Lancashire. In 1972 the *Ormskirk Advertiser* was bought to fortify the western flank.

This watching of essential interest, this deliberate planning with an end in view, and prompt rejection of the irrelevant, lies at the core of United's progress. Its board is nicely balanced between men with newspaper expertise, both editorial and commercial, and men with wide practical knowledge of business and finance. It was strengthened in 1974 by the addition of Mr D. R. Stevens, representing the interest of the Drayton Group Today the company stands in a position of formidable strength. In the words of the Press Council survey already quoted, 'It is now big enough to undertake any publishing venture it wishes—and is one of the very few newspaper groups in whose managerial talents the Stock Exchange has any confidence.'

The most immediate and important 'publishing venture' that lies ahead of United is the building and equipment of new premises to house the Northampton papers. Work has now begun. Some £5 million will be expended on offices and works which will incorporate web-offset and other modern processes, enabling the *Chronicle and Echo* and the *Mercury and Herald* to meet the needs of that phenomenally-developing area with efficient productions of the highest quality.

The United premises will be among the most attractively designed and arresting landmarks in the new Northampton.

SOME NOTABLE DATES

1918	United Newspapers Ltd. founded
1927	Company sold by Mr Lloyd George
1928	Acquired by Mr William Harrison
1929	Provincial Newspapers Ltd. established
1929	Harrison eclipsed in Inveresk crisis.
1930	Mr Herbert Brent Grotrian becomes chairman
1930	*Daily Chronicle* merged in *Daily News*
1936	United sells its share in *News Chronicle*
1947	Company taken over by Drayton interests
1948	Mr H. C. Drayton assumes chairmanship
1948	Mr W. D. Barnetson joins *Edinburgh Evening News*
1963	United sells its share in *Hull Daily Mail* to Lord Rothermere
1963	Sheffield Newspapers acquired
1963	*Yorkshire Evening News* sold to Yorkshire Post Newspapers and closed down
1964	Blackpool newspapers acquired
1966	Death of Harley Drayton; Mr Barnetson succeeds
1966	*Doncaster Evening Post* founded
1969	United purchase Bradbury Agnew Ltd., and *Punch*
1969	Merger, by acquisition, with Yorkshire Post Newspapers.

PART TWO: THE BOUGHS

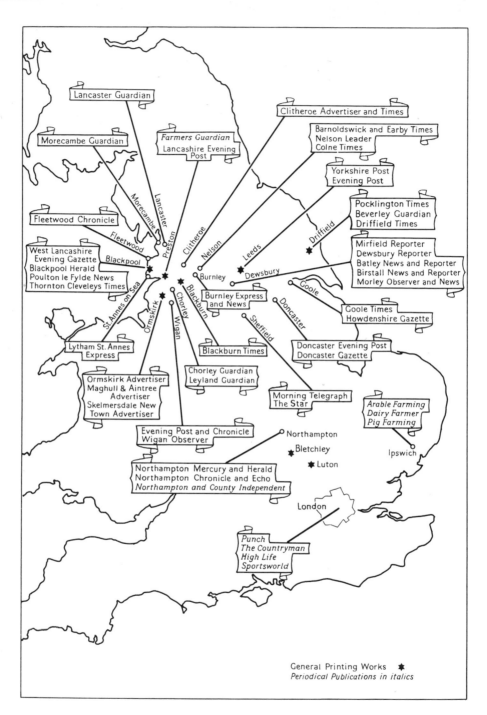

Lancaster Guardian

Clitheroe Advertiser and Times

Morecambe Guardian

Farmers Guardian
Lancashire Evening
Post

Barnoldswick and Earby Times
Nelson Leader
Colne Times

Yorkshire Post
Evening Post

Fleetwood Chronicle

Pocklington Times
Beverley Guardian
Driffield Times

West Lancashire
Evening Gazette
Blackpool Herald
Poulton le Fylde News
Thornton Cleveleys Times

Mirfield Reporter
Dewsbury Reporter
Batley News and Reporter
Birstall News and Reporter
Morley Observer and News

Burnley Express
and News

Goole Times
Howdenshire Gazette

Lytham St. Annes
Express

Blackburn Times

Ormskirk Advertiser
Maghull & Aintree
Advertiser
Skelmersdale New
Town Advertiser

Chorley Guardian
Leyland Guardian

Doncaster Evening Post
Doncaster Gazette

Morning Telegraph
The Star

Arable Farming
Dairy Farmer
Pig Farming

Evening Post and Chronicle
Wigan Observer

Northampton
Bletchley
Luton

Ipswich

Northampton Mercury and Herald
Northampton Chronicle and Echo
Northampton and County Independent

London

Punch
The Countryman
High Life
Sportsworld

General Printing Works ✸
Periodical Publications in italics

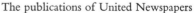

The publications of United Newspapers

62

1

HOW THEY WORK

EACH newspaper owned by United is managed and edited on the spot by men who have come to belong to the place where *it* belongs and know the requirements and characteristics of the people. Most of the editors are men either born in, or long familiar with, the towns and shires where they work. So, too, in general, are the staffs who report the news and gather the advertisements.

All United's newspapers are in the provinces. Some of them are important journals published in teeming cities, but whether this be the case or whether they are serving small market towns they have their roots in a region with a distinctive life and a precise experience, and their viability depends on the faithfulness with which they reflect these, not only in the coverage of events but in the formulation of views.

If Leeds, Sheffield, Northampton and Preston are expected to display a more emphatic interest in national and international affairs than is required of a little weekly it is important that their assessments should take into account (though, of course, not necessarily having to advocate) what their great communities are manifesting in their reaction to the subject under discussion. In this way a regional and local Press contributes valuably to the formation of national opinion.

Every United editor is free to print what he deems to be proper, subject only to the law. If he feels he should condemn the Government he will do so. If he has cause to utter lamentations about the quality of the local water—or the beer for that matter—nobody on high is going to stop him. If his mayor happens to be a shareholder in United his Worship will not therefore avoid the critical scrutiny to which all who hold public office must submit.

Nor is this a question of journalistic ethics alone; it is the only course of conduct that ensures a newspaper's prosperity and consequentially the prosperity of the group to which it may belong.

There are critics who are suspicious of newspaper groups. Why should a lot of newspapers be gathered together under one umbrella, they ask. Is it not against the public interest that large segments of the Press should be controlled by companies based on London? These critics fail to realise that a newspaper is a body composed of two main elements. It is a medium for the diffusion of news and information—or 'intelligence' as our forbears called it—and it is also a business, dependent on the inflow of money and wise economic administration. As just emphasised, there is no control from headquarters of the 'intelligence', the editorial content, of the various papers. Each editor is as free as ever his predecessors were when they were locally owned—indeed, more so, for in the old days proprietors were often deeply involved in local politics and commerce whereas the directors of a large company like United are indifferent to such interests.

The London editorial staff at Tudor Street are the servants, not the masters, of the editors in the provinces. What they distribute by way of news is at the disposal of the editors, to be 'spiked' or to be published. The decision is never London's. But London's contribution is very important.

Drew Webster, a former chairman of the Parliamentary Lobby Journalists, is the London Editor of the group, while Robert Scott, also a former Lobby correspondent, is London Editor of the *Yorkshire Post* and *Morning Telegraph*. Together with their reporters and specialists they supply the papers with a flow of material of national concern, covering politics and diplomacy, finance, defence, farming, crime and metropolitan entertainment. Sport is a consequential activity of the London Office and group newspapers receive their own staff coverage of events like the Olympic Games, the World Cup and the Commonwealth Games.

It is in the realm of administration that a group justifies itself. Administration is not editing: it is the control and deployment of resources, the selection of priorities, the planning of future development. Grouping means this: that the resources of the strong are there for the defence of the weak, and the weak may thereby be so helped that they come to stand on their own feet. A newspaper group is a newspaper commonwealth. There are today newspapers serving their communities in lively and efficient fashion that, but for the cover provided by a group, would have disappeared owing to the pressures of economic change.

Now to look at the histories of papers which belong to the United commonwealth. There are two morning dailies, seven evening dailies, thirty-two weeklies and eight periodicals, as follow:

MORNINGS

Yorkshire Post	*Morning Telegraph* (Sheffield)

EVENINGS

Evening Post (Leeds)	*The Star* (Sheffield)
Lancashire Evening Post	*Chronicle & Echo*
West Lancashire Evening	(Northampton)
Gazette	*Doncaster Evening Post*
Evening Post and Chronicle (Wigan)	

WEEKLIES

Barnoldswick and Earby Times	*Batley News and Reporter*
Beverley Guardian	*Birstall News*
Blackburn Times	*Blackpool Gazette and Herald*
Burnley Express & News	*Chorley Guardian*
Clitheroe Advertiser & Times	*Colne Times*
Dewsbury Reporter & District	*Doncaster Gazette*
News	*Driffield Times*
Fleetwood Chronicle	*Goole Times*
Lancaster Guardian	*Howdenshire Gazette*
Leyland Guardian	*Lytham St Annes Express*
Mercury & Herald	*Mirfield Reporter*
(Northampton)	*Morley Observer & News*
Maghull and Aintree	*Pocklington Times*
Advertiser	*Skelmersdale Advertiser*
Morecambe Guardian	*Nelson Leader*

Ormskirk Advertiser   *Wigan Observer*
Poulton-le-Fylde News   *Thornton Cleveleys Times*

PERIODICALS

Punch   *The Countryman*
Northampton & County   *Sportsworld*
   Independent   *Dairy Farmer*
Arable Farming   *Pig Farming*
Farmers Guardian

2

CIIYMISTRY AND CULTURE

DOWN in Huntingdonshire the venerable ones drew spellbound audiences when they told how they had seen him with their very own eyes—the Lord Protector Noll Cromwell, the old sojer himself. Younger folk, not to be outdone, were beginning to declare that they had come across his ghost, in buff jacket and breastplate, haunting its native meads at twilight. It was the beginning of the Eighteenth Century.

And at that time down in Huntingdonshire—at St Ives to be precise—a young man more representative of a new era was applying his wits to contemporary developments. The *news*, printed intelligence—that was the thing for the enterprising to go for. The young man was Robert Raikes. He had the right ideas but he was not very business-like, being rather bookish and meditative, so he sought him a practical partner and found the answer in young William Dicey. Master Dicey belonged to a family that was determined to make money. Pills, cordials, purges and plasters were the things the Diceys sold, in collaboration with a London 'chymist' named Sutton.

Raikes and Dicey put their heads together and founded the *St Ives Postboy*, hoping to sell intelligence and pills by one and the same operation; but somehow the paper hung fire. The pills went all right but not the *Postboy*. So, after a year or two, they cast about for a more lively and appreciative place than St Ives, and their eyes fell on Northampton, only forty miles away. Nobody was selling intelligence in Northampton and there were plenty of innards there to be galvanised by purges.

It was Dicey who took his nag and rode over the miry ways to

VOL. I.   NUMB. 1.

Northampton *Mercury,*
OR THE
MONDAY's POST.
BEING A
Collection of the most Material Occurrences,

Foreign & Domestick.

Together with
An Account of Trade.

MONDAY, May 2, 1720. [*To be continued weekly.*]

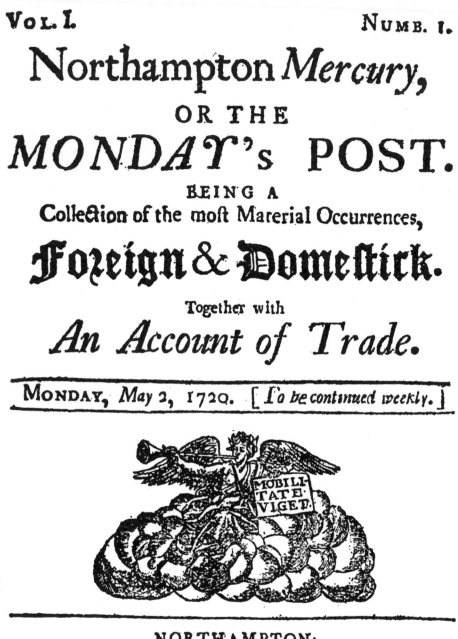

NORTHAMPTON:
Printed by *R. Raikes* and *W. Dicey,* near *All Saints Church;* where
Advertisements and Letters of Correspondents are taken in, and all
manner of Books printed.

Issue number one of the *Northampton Mercury* published on May 2, 1720

Northampton in order as they say, to 'case the joint'. He was delighted with the reception accorded by the principal burgesses and reported back to Raikes that prospects seemed good. So in due time there appeared before the fascinated eyes of the Northampton public a bang up-to-date phenomenon calling itself the *Northampton Mercury or the Monday's Post, being a Collection of the most Material Occurences, Foreign and Domestick, together with an Account of Trade (to be continued Weekly).*

The first issue was published on Monday, May 2 1720. It has 'continued weekly' without a break ever since. For the first few years it functioned at George Row, Northampton, but about 1730 it moved to more spacious premises in The Parade. And there in The Parade (though next door) it is still produced. The *Mercury* is 255 years old and for over 240 years it has had the same address, The Parade, Northampton. Surely that is a world record for any newspaper. One suspects another record in proprietorship. The Dicey family continued to own and edit the paper until 1885, a span of 165 years.

Some time after its foundation Robert Raikes departed from the scene. He went to seek further fortune in Gloucestershire and there he fathered another Robert Raikes who, when he came to man's estate, pioneered Sunday Schools and earned for himself a statue in the Embankment gardens.

But how did young William Dicey make the *Mercury* 'tick' from the very day it started? By the oldest method known to commerce. He ensured that it was consistently a jump ahead. In those days it was customary to depend on the lumbering stage-coaches to bring the latest broadsheets and news-letters from London. This was not good enough for Dicey. He employed sturdy Northamptonshire lads, mounted on fleet steeds, to outpace the coaches. Accoutred with plenty of loaded pistols to discharge at interfering highwaymen, they went to London, collared the necessary sheets of intelligence, and galloped back along the sixty miles to Northampton, beating the coaches by as much as four hours. By the time the mail arrived the *Mercury* had been printed and its postboys were on their way to scatter it all over the neighbouring shires. At the same time they scattered pills, for, as announcements in the *Mercury* made plain, the medicaments of the Dicey-Sutton combine were always available

MONDAY, *May 22, 1721.* [*To be continued Weekly.*]

NORTHAMPTON:

Printed by R. RAIKES and W. DICEY, near ALL SAINTS CHURCH,
where Advertifements are taken in, and all manner of Books are fairly
printed, or neatly bound, gilt, and letter'd, in Sheep, Calf, Vellum,
Turkey or Morocco. Where alfo may be had Land Tax Receipts, Affeſ-
fors Warrants, Funeral Affidavits, &c. Likewife all manner of Statio-
nary Ware, as Shop-Books, Pocket-Books, Paper, Pens, Ink, Wax, &c.

(Price of the Mercury Three Half Pence.)

Vol. 2 No. 4 of the *Northampton Mercury*

THE Northampton Mercury

MONDAY, *June* 28, 1725. [*To be continued Weekly.*]

GOODS Imported and Exported at the Port of *London*, from *June* 8, to *June* 15, 1725.

[*IMPORTED*] 840 Kid-Skins, 4357 Deer-Skins, 1730 Fox, 734 Mink, 1216 Raccoon, 28 Bear, 1234 Beaver, 354 Mufquash, from *Cadiz, New-England, New-York,* &c.—497 Casks, 43 Chests Wine, 12 Tons, 1070 Gallons Brandy, 1020 Gallons Rum, 34 Baskets Spaw-Water; 51 Tons, 61 Gallons Oil, from *Lisbon, Leghorn, Holland,* &c.—30707 Ells Linnen, 109330 Yards ditto, 600 Lawns, 312 Cambricks, 1000 Ells Canvas, 4500 Ells Holland Duck, 122 Ticks, 448 Burdens, from *Holland Dublin, Bridges, Dantzick, Oftend, Turkey,* &c.—1250 l. Nutmegs, 400 l. Cloves, 1230 l. Cinnamon, from *Holland,* &c.—49 Tons Logwood, 420 l. Cochineal, 1547 l. Indico, from *Rhode-Island, Cadiz,* &c.—470 Hogsheads Tobacco, from *Virginia, Carolina,* &c.

[*EXPORTED.*] 3000 Ounces For. Gold, 20000 Oz. For. Silver, 000 Oz Plate, 11 C. Brafs, 8 C Copper, 75 C. Pewter, 000 C. Tin, 387 C. Lead, 240 C. Wrought Iron, 125 C. Leather, 230 l. Shoes, 1650 Quarters Wheat, 000 Quarters Wheatmeal, 15 C. Bisket, 140 Quarters Rye, 000 Quarters Barley, 30 Quarters Beans, 40 Groce Pipes, 000 C. Hops, 11 Tons Beer, 6 C. Haberdashery, to *Holland, France, Spain, Germany the Straits, Newfoundland, Cork,* &c. — 3289 Stuffs, 20 Says, 60 Serges, 990 Perpets, 147 Kersies, 508 Double Bays, 26 Single Bays, 472 Minikin Bays, 100 Long Cloths, 27 Short Cloths, 11 Spanish Cloths, 14330 Yards Flannel, 1310 Goads Cotton, 2125 Doz. Hose 145 Doz. Castors, 30 Doz. Felts, to *Holland, Spain, Legborn, Messina, Bremen, Norway, W Indies,* &c. 14 Ships entred inwards, and 14 clear'd out.

The WEEKLY BILL of MORTALITY, from *June* 15, to *June* 22, 1725.

AGED — 34	Cough — 1	Loofnefs — 1	Rifing of the Lights — 3	Teeth — 20
Apoplexy — 1	Dropfie — 20	Mortification — 3	Rupure — 1	Thrush — 2
Asthma — 1	Fever — 57	Palfie — 1	Small-Pox — 84	Tiffick — 2
Child-bed — 5	French-Pox — 2	Plurifie — 1	Stilborn — 11	Water in the Head — 1
Colick — 1	Griping in the Guts — 14	Purples — 2	Stoppage in the Stomach 2	
Confumption — 56	Horfhochead — 2	Rafh — 1	Strangury — 1	
Convulfion — 116	Jaundies — 2	Rickets — 2	Suddenly — 3	

CASUALTIES. Drowned accidentally in the River of Thames 3. One buried at St. Andrew in Holborn, One at St. Catherine by the Tower, and one at St. Margarets Westminster. Kill'd by a Fall from a Scaffold at Alhallows in Lombard-street. (buried at St. Helen's near Bishopfgate) 1.
Christned 352. Buried 458. Increafed in the Burials this Week 23.

Vol. 5 No. 9 of the *Northampton Mercury*

from 'the men that carry this news.'

Later in the Eighteenth Century the *Northampton Mercury* developed into the most widely-circulated paper in the kingdom. Packages went by coach to Derby, Sheffield, Hull, York, Durham and Newcastle; to Chester and Liverpool; to Leicester, Coventry and Birmingham; to Lichfield, Peterborough, Cambridge, Norwich, Ipswich, Oxford, Reading and Gloucester. It took a world-wide view of the news. Its greatest 'scoop' was during the 1745 rebellion.

Bonnie-Prince Charlie and his Highlanders were plunging deep into England. When they reached Derby the *Mercury* rushed to press with a special edition for things were getting hot. Soldiers were arriving at Northampton, ready to give battle on Harlestone Heath. Then came a messenger from the North; he galloped to The Parade with the news that Charles Stuart's gallant but ragged army had decided to pack up and go home; the retreat had begun.

71

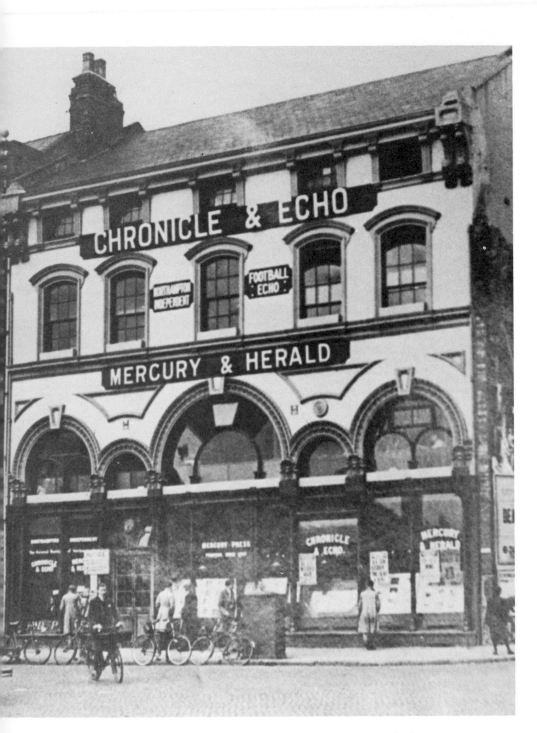

The original building at Northampton

Two early *Northampton Herald* mastheads

Another special edition was whipped to press and it was the *Northampton Mercury* which, ahead of all rivals, told England that the last invasion of her territory was over. One need not doubt that the glad tidings were accompanied by pills ensuring that de-costivation coincided with the general relief.

In 1757 William Dicey was succeeded as editor by his son, Cluer Dicey, who became a well-known figure not only in the Midlands and in London but over many counties, for his paper was by then *the* newspaper to half the readers of provincial England. It was first in the field with cartoons—'a hundred and twenty years ahead of *Punch*', as one of its zealots has written—and it pioneered the use of maps to illustrate the news. Its extensive account of the battle of Dettingen (1743) remains a classic of early journalism.

Thomas Dicey followed Cluer, then his son, Thomas Edward Dicey. By now the family were wealthy and lived in style. In the 1830s James de Wilde began an editorship which spanned forty years, till his death in 1871. Fourteen years later the Diceys abandoned the paper and it was taken over by a former member of the staff, Samuel Smith Campion. He was a dynamo of a man and quickly restored its failing health. He snapped up new devices almost as soon as they were invented. The *Mercury* claims that under his control it became the first paper to introduce rotary presses, the first to use electric power and light, the first to install linotype machines and the first to have a photo engraving plant.

Its most celebrated editor was William Waite Hadley under whose brilliant direction the *Mercury* not only forged ahead but consistently outpointed a rival that had been operating for many years, the *Northampton Herald*. In later life Hadley edited, and in great measure created, the modern *Sunday Times* from which he only retired when he was 84. But he had left his indelible mark in Northampton and presently the *Mercury* absorbed its competitor and adopted its present title, *Mercury and Herald*.

During that period the town's other papers, the *Northampton Daily Chronicle*, the *Echo* and the *Independent* were combined into a group under the control of Provincial Newspapers Ltd. A few years ago the *Mercury and Herald* was refashioned in contemporary style, and its editor, Kenneth Nutt conducts it with vigour and native sagacity. He is fortunate to have as a contributor Mr L. W. Dickens who edited the paper for 27 years.

The *Mercury* has always kept abreast of changing times, but it is inevitable that a paper with such a length of years should draw one back to its earliest files. In that first issue of May 2 1720 there is plenty to rivet the attention. The weekly Bill of Mortality tells us that the chief causes of death were 'convulsions' and 'fevers'; that nine died from 'griping of the guts', two from 'rising of the lights', five 'suddenly', and one from 'teeth.'

A message from the Hague discloses the interesting fact that Cardinal Alberoni 'had 12 millions at one time in the Bank of Geneva', suggesting that the Swiss gnomes were as active then as now. The South Sea Company 'open'd Books this day for new Subscriptions for a million at 400 per cent.' Another item says: 'Last week the Oxford stage-coach was robb'd between Uxbridge and London by the same Highwaymen, as is supposed, who robb'd the Bristol Mail.'

NORTHAMPTON, THURSDAY, OCTOBER 3, 1974 ● 3p

The Northampton *Mercury & Herald* masthead, 1974

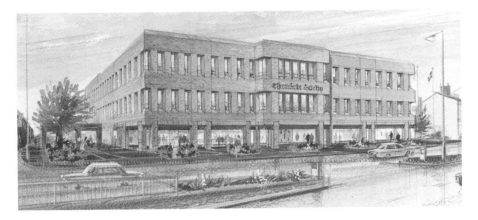

The new building at Northampton

Eighteenth Century editors were charmingly indifferent to libel and contempt of court. 'Elizabeth Canbury', we read, 'is try'd this day for poisoning her father near Twickenham by putting Arsnick in his Milk-porridge; the fact is pretty plain and is now under the Jury's Consideration.' Two days later the sinister lady was condemned to death, but it then appears that she had not poisoned her father but her father-in-law—which might be said to make all the difference.

Local correspondents had a shrewd sense of news values. They were quick to report that species of wonder which in all centuries never fails to open eyes of amazement, beside which lunar modules and infra-red rays are but passing phenomena. In an early issue the *Mercury* reveals that 'one Richard Adams of Farthingo has a Crop of Turnips now quite ripe, one row whereof now growing is 50 inches about. He has likewise a Carrott of 7 foot and 3 quarters high and 20 inches round.'

Whether it was the *Mercury* or the chymistry that lifted the Diceys into opulence is now beyond ascertainment, but the two interests continued to be fused for some 150 years. Only by reproducing a typical advertisement in the fullness of its text can justice be done to so famous and protracted an exercise in promotion. The reproduction appears on page viii. Well into the last century the campaign was still pulsating through the villages of Fenland, where printed cards bearing this poem were to be seen in shop windows:

> *Daffy's Elixer, hot and spicey,*
> *Made by Sutton, sold by Dicey.*

75

Two other journals now belonging to the United group were born in the Eighteenth Century. One is the *Yorkshire Post* (1754) but that renowned newspaper requires the next chapter to itself. The other is the *Doncaster Gazette*, which first appeared in 1786.

Immediately, and in some mystification, one comes upon pills again. For the worthy who founded the *Doncaster Gazette* as the *Yorkshire Journal and General Weekly Advertiser* on an August day in 1786 was one Thomas Sanderson, a chymist. He also used his paper for advertising his wares. He specialised in liquorice, and it is important to bear in mind that the world-renowned liquorice fields of Pontefract (honoured in our own day by Sir John Betjeman) were but a few miles from Doncaster. He was also as conscious as modern TV advertisers of the need to keep bringing in something 'new'. At one stage he confessed that his 'balsam of liquorice root' was not altogether convenient for travellers, but the use of his '*refined* liquorice root', he assured them, would be in every way as efficacious. This preparation he especially recommended to 'gentlemen of the pulpit, bar and army' and others who were required to speak in public. They would find that its ingredients, being 'perfectly free from all impurities', would help them in 'distinctness of utterance.'

Thomas Sanderson, a councilman of Doncaster, took a far geographical horizon for his paper. From the start it had distribution points in all parts of Yorkshire and north Nottinghamshire. What is more, Sanderson was determined that London should also have the benefit of his news and views. The 'Editor's agent' in the capital was to be found at 5 Warwick Square, Newgate Street, and copies of the *Journal* were placed in the Chapter Coffee House in Paternoster Row and at Peele's Coffee House in Fleet Street. (It is only within the last year or two that Peele's sandwich bar, the successor to that establishment, has sadly come to an end.)

But Sanderson did not live long to enjoy his expanding enterprise; in 1790 he died. The last item penned by this first editor, who was long remembered in the district for his kindness, courtesy and public spirit, was about an 'elegant entertainment' given by a newly-elected member of Doncaster common council. It concluded: 'May every guest on future similar occasions cultivate the same spirit of cheerfulness, good nature and brotherly love

Doncaster Journal,
AND
YORKSHIRE ADVERTISER.

PRINTED BY E. SANDERSON.

SATURDAY, December 3, 1791.   [PRIC

The Doncaster Gazette.

FRIDAY, FEBRUARY 10, 1882.   (ESTABLISHED IN 1786.)   PRICE 2D.—VOL. LXXXIX.—No. 4,980.

The *Doncaster Gazette*, 1791 and 1882

as appeared to actuate all on that joyous night; then, while smiling pleasure and calm content crown the flowing bowl, the pestilent breath of dissension shall never offend us more.'

There then happened an event which affords Doncaster a special niche in journalistic annals. Sanderson's widow, 'agreeable to the dying request of her deceased husband', took over the *Journal* and edited and managed it for some years with vigour and originality. Was Elizabeth Sanderson the first woman editor of a newspaper? At all events she showed the men how to do it; she was highly ingenious in promoting advertisements and when, four years later, there appeared a competitor, the *Yorkshire Nottinghamshire and Lincolnshire Gazette*, she immediately pointed out to her readers that she had put into the *Journal* 'four additional columns.' What she did not mention was that each of the five columns on a page of this refashioned *Journal* was three eighths of an inch narrower than each of the four columns on a page of the old. Elizabeth knew a thing or two.

The young man who had started the rival *Gazette* in January 1794 was destined to play an outstanding part in the affairs of Doncaster, in due time holding office as mayor. Besides operating a newspaper he managed to be the town's Postmaster, circulated

Doncaster Gazette

No. 9802   Thursday, September 26, 1974   Established 1786.   (Incorporating The Doncaster Chronicle)   **Price 3p**   Tel: 4001

THE PAPER FOR THE YOUNG AT HEART

The *Doncaster Gazette*, 1974

as an insurance agent, and was a leading auctioneer. Inevitably he also sold pills. His name was William Sheardown. Three years after founding the *Gazette*, on the demise of the doughty Elizabeth Sanderson, he absorbed her *Journal* and thereby found himself with a newspaper monopoly in Doncaster. As he wrote percipiently in the *Gazette:* 'The increase of Readers from the decline of the Doncaster Journal in our favour we consider as a material Advantage to our Advertising Friends.'

More than once during the next century the *Gazette* played about with its title, endeavouring to identify itself with the three counties in which it circulated. At one time it reached the monstrous redundancy of *Doncaster, Nottingham and Lincoln Gazette, and Yorkshire, Nottinghamshire and Lincolnshire Advertiser*, and it was not until 1882 that some sensible fellow crisped things down to *Doncaster Gazette*, the name it has borne ever since.

The Sheardown family, fathers and sons, presided over its destiny from 1794 until 1827, when it was sold, together with their printing and bookselling business, to Messrs T. Brooke and Co. Mr Thomas Brooke had worked for the Sheardowns; his son succeeded him and subsequently families named White and Hatfield were linked with the Brookes in the conduct of the paper. They were no Tories. The *Gazette* stood valiantly for the Reform Bill and was a staunch supporter of John Bright.

Again, in 1893, the paper changed hands. It was acquired by Mr Joseph Cooke, a Lincolnshire journalist who was a bit of a Roy Thomson in his generation and at various times owned the *Sheffield Independent* and the *Morning Herald* of London. Finally, in 1925, it came under the wing of United as part of Provincial Newspapers Ltd. Today it is an impressive example of weekly journalism, printing the news and watching the interests of an important town. Its editor, Mr Kenneth Dutton, has given a quarter of a century of devoted service to his paper and his community.

As in the case of the Northampton *Mercury*, it is to the quaint

78

items that the modern reader turns when he looks at the early files. Surely this deserves a prize among wedding reports: 'Mr Todd, shoemaker, to Miss Maria Wright. The bride and bridegroom had but one pair of legs between them, and each sported a new timber toe on the occasion—the bridesmaid was lame and blind of an eye and the father was lame and deaf.' In 1817 the *Gazette* reported: 'On Monday morning at the butter cross in this town the passive wife of a journeyman tailer was conducted by her husband, amidst a concourse of the gazing population, to the public Cross where, after placing a halter round her neck, he disposed of his fair rib—or rather spare rib— to an admiring painter at the moderate price of five shillings and sixpence. O Tempora! O Mores!'

There is a certain astringency in this piece of exclusive news:

> We understand that Miss Swinnerton, of Bullerton Hall near Newcastle, will in a few weeks be led to the hymeneal altar by Sir W. Pilkington, Bart., of Wakefield. In addition to a most amiable disposition, polished manners, and refinement, her fortune is calculated to exceed £110,000.

Then the eye falls on a pathetic little burial notice, its implications standing in bitter contrast with the elegance of Miss Swinnerton's *milieu:* 'July 30. Sarah Goulding, an apprentice to the worsted manufactory, aged 9 years, of fever.' (1800).

The old yellow pages of such provincial papers unfold history with a breadth of range and a disregard for contrivance that is not found in more studied literary works. They reflect innumerable facets of the mortal pilgrimage; as we turn them, decade by decade, we note the purblind, halting, yet definitive movement of social evolution as it is manifest in the endeavours, the sufferings, the enjoyments—even the stupidities—of ordinary people and extraordinary characters.

Those papers took the world for their parish. They were the only media of 'intelligence, foreign and domestick' then available. They were read beside candles that glimmered hundreds of miles from where they were printed. Cumulatively they hold a national record more important than that of the more inward-looking London newspapers which existed in the Eighteenth and early Nineteenth centuries. And how often, in scanning them, one is forced to exclaim, 'There's nothing new under the sun!'

In 1825, for example, the *Doncaster Gazette* published this piece of information:

> A new company is about to be established for the purpose of opening a communication by means of a tunnel under the British Channel between Dover and Calais. The capital will amount to £270,000,000 14s. 5¼d., and the shareholders will comprise the principal capitalists of both countries. This stupendous work is to be styled the Anglo-Gallic Grand International Junction Channel of Communication.

THE *YORKSHIRE POST*

MOST people know that Yorkshire is the biggest county in England, but not so many realise just how big it is. Were you to join together Kent, Sussex, Surrey, Essex, Hertfordshire and Bedfordshire you would have reached little more than the acreage of Yorkshire. Therefore Yorkshire deems itself a province commanding the nation's ear to a unique extent; and the newspaper that speaks for it, and in every characteristic epitomises it, is the *Yorkshire Post*. Its influence upon the affairs of the kingdom is a matter of history; on vital issues in commerce and politics it has wielded persuasive authority, and at times of national and international crisis it has more than once been decisive.

The strength of the *Yorkshire Post* lies not in a circulation of millions but in three cardinal assets. It is completely identified with the great province which has sustained it for more than two hundred years; it is detached from the atmosphere of the capital; it holds a political philosophy that it has wrought for itself out of principles ratified by experience.

The *Yorkshire Post* will never move itself to London, deluded by a false notion that Fleet Street is the only point of vantage from which to address the nation. To do so would be not only to sacrifice its birthright but—as it sees it—to be handicapped by having to function amid those debilitating concentrations of trend, topic and political 'intellectualism' which are typical of all seats of government. Similarly, its openly-avowed Toryism is not necessarily that which happens to prevail at Westminster. It goes deeper than the requirements of expediency or Party conflict; it is rooted in human values. It is the 'radical' blend of

Conservatism exemplified by Shaftesbury and Michael Thomas Sadler. The *Yorkshire Post* fought for reform against the mercantile dictators of the industrial revolution. It fought for shorter hours for manual workers, for the abolition of child labour, for the early closing of shops.

Robert Perring, who edited the *Yorkshire Post* in the 1830s, gave his paper a motto: 'The Altar, the Throne and the Cottage.' (Not, you will notice, 'the Mansion'.) The motto has never really been superseded. A hundred years later when, to the dismay of many people, the *Yorkshire Post* led the way in unfolding those events which resulted in the abdication of Edward VIII, it was the Throne which it conceived to be in danger.

From these claims and assertions it might be imagined that the *Yorkshire Post* operates in a climate of self-diffusing state and circumstance. Not so—as Lord Beaverbrook would have said. It is neither pretentious nor sanctimonious; it displays no phylactery. It wears its portion of scholarship modestly and is as much at home with other modest people and their bingo as it is with the knights of the shire and their grouse.

Yet if there is no place for the prig in Yorkshire and community among men of all degrees is highly regarded there, it must be confessed that the *Yorkshire Post*, like Yorkshiremen in general, is guilty of a deception that has gained world-wide currency—the pretence that they are a hard, unemotional, call-a-spade-a-bloody-shovel kind of people. Beneath this propaganda they try to hide its antithesis, their real characteristic, but unwittingly they fail. It is a characteristic of the *Yorkshire Post* and marks that paper off from other journals of its stature. It was first identified to the English-speaking world—nay, in a word was invented—by a Yorkshire parson.

During the early years of the *Yorkshire Post* the vicar of Sutton-in-the-Forest, near York, was that ecclesiastic extraordinary the Rev. Laurence Sterne, soon to be renowned as the author of *Tristram Shandy*. Sometime around 1740 he had sat down in his sweetheart's abode, in Little Alice Lane near York Minster, and bemoaned her absence as he gazed upon the table laid for supper:

> One solitary plate, one knife, one fork, one glass!—I gave a thousand pensive, penetrating looks at the chair thou hadst so often graced in those quiet and sentimental

> repasts—then laid down my knife and fork, and took out my handkerchief, and clapped it across my face, and wept like a child!

The lachrymosity in this letter may be put aside as typical Sterne eyewash; the important thing to note is the one word 'sentimental.' For this was the first time it had ever been used.

How had it arrived? What genius brought it into being? From what depth of his soul had Sterne dredged it up? He slapped it into that letter and in no time it was to be heard all over the land, yet nobody seems to have known what it meant. In 1749 Lady Bradshaigh wrote to Samuel Richardson the novelist, asking him if he could define 'the meaning of the word *sentimental*, so much in vogue among the polite . . .'[1]

Well, for the edification of the polite let it be said that the word means something which is persistently inherent in Laurence Sterne's compatriots, fain as they are to disavow it. It means a poignant awareness of the essence of life stripped of all artifice, deprived of all disguise and particularity; a zest for every human commonplace, whereof the kiss and the clout, melancholy and merriment, grace and grief are the alternating currents. In short, a responsiveness of heart, a sympathy with universal frailty and folly through acknowledgement of one's own.

He who is astute enough to look below the surface will find that, in this correct sense, there is more *sentiment* to a page of the *Yorkshire Post* than in whole volumes of some of its peers who are more conscious of cerebellum than bloodstream.

The *Yorkshire Post* was founded as the *Leeds Intelligencer* on July 2 1754. Its proprietor was a certain Griffith Wright and he and his son between them edited it for the first half century of its spirited existence. It is perhaps unnecessary by now to say that the family also sold pills; indeed, the *Leeds Intelligencer* was odoriferous of the pharmacy. Puffs for Wright medicaments appeared regularly, and when in 1818 the family disposed of it to three gentlemen named Kirkby, Gawtrees and Inchbold we read that they traded under the title Gawtrees and Co., 'which subsisted to sell patent medicines as well as to engage in printing.'

[1]See Peter Quennell's study of Sterne in *Four Portraits*.

THE
LEEDES INTELLIGENCER.

Printed by GRIFFITH WRIGHT, in the LOWER-HEAD-ROW.

N° I.　　　　　TUESDAY, *July* 2, 1754.

The PUBLISHER's PREFACE.

First issue of the *Leeds Intelligencer*, July 2, 1754

When the first Mr Wright began his venture he was a brave man, for there was already a vigorous newspaper in the town, the *Leeds Mercury*, which had been founded nearly forty years before. Between the *Intelligencer* and the *Mercury* there developed a warfare for which there are few parallels in the annals of journalism. Never was the eloquence of rudery more gloriously wielded. Guerilla tactics sufficed during the early phases of the campaign, the *Mercury* noting with acidulous satisfaction such mishaps as the printing of a word upside down in its competitor. But when Mr Edward Baines took over the *Mercury* in 1801 the temperature rose rapidly.

Baines, who was destined to build his newspaper into a great Whig-Liberal force in the North, did not lack aggression. When he kept claiming that the *Mercury* had a circulation far in excess of any other paper in the town of Leeds, the *Intelligencer*, as the *only* other one, was stung into retorts like this

> The late ostentatious vaunting, puffing and pother of a neighbouring Printer, about himself and his paper, must have strongly reminded his readers of the aspiring bloated frog in the fable . . . And what is the result of all this vain boaster's gasconading? Nothing more than what was before perfectly well-known, viz., that the circulation of the *Mercury* is confined to the disaffected and the illiterate, who are easily misled, deceived and

84

cajoled by flattery and the abuse of their governors.

Having made a profit of just over £400 in four years, the Gawtrees organisation tired of the *Leeds Intelligencer* and in 1822 got rid of it to two gentlemen better equipped with the necessary qualifications, Joseph Ogle Robinson and John Hernaman. Robinson belonged to an old Leeds family with literary interests and Hernaman was an experienced newspaper man. The first thing they did was to appoint a young and energetic editor, Alaric Watts.

Watts was only 25 but during his three years as editor he gave the paper a touch of new distinction and slanted it against any suspicion that it might be the organ of ruthless tycoonery. After seeing for himself the conditions prevailing in the industrial West Riding he commented strongly on the inhumanity of mill-owners, receiving 'as many letters discontinuing subscriptions as filled a breakfast tray.' He was the last man to worry about that even though his proprietors were more than a little concerned. Inevitably he went for Baines of the *Mercury* and had the distinction of winning a shilling from him by way of libel damages.

On more general considerations Alaric Watts is entitled to a few paragraphs. He was versatile, enterprising, ingenious; he must have been an engaging chap to meet. He had been in turn a school usher, a tutor in the family of Signor Ruspini, dentist to the Prince Regent, 'who maintained a handsome establishment in Pall Mall', and then briefly a flautist. He appeared once at the Royal Opera House in pantaloons tied with ribbon at the ankles. Journalism came next and in a surprisingly short time we find him editor of the *New Monthly Magazine*. He met Ogle Robinson in London and was lured to the editorship of the *Leeds Intelligencer* by a salary of £300 a year.

When he went to Leeds in 1823 he took with him a lovely wife, a Quakeress who had had to sever herself from the Society of Friends in order to marry him. There exist two memorable tributes to her charms. 'What shoulders that child has!' cried the elderly Duchess of Bedford on meeting her in the park at Woburn, while no less an authority than Sir Thomas Lawrence, the great portrait painter, having watched her turning over some prints in a shop, exclaimed to a friend, 'I have today seen a lady with the most beautiful hands I ever saw.' One can imagine the

Henry Howard, R.A.

Anna Lea Merritt.

Alaric Watts, editor of the *Leeds Intelligencer* from 1822 to 1825. Portrait by Henry Howard, R.A. Reproduced from the biography written by his son in 1884.

twitterings among the matrons of Leeds when they looked upon Mrs Watts, whose 'liquid blue eyes', we are told, lent radiance to a 'Madonna-like face.'

Her husband may not have been a heavyweight in his time but he was an effective lightweight. He wrote poetry in Byron's more sentimental manner and it drew commendation from Wordsworth, Coleridge and Charles Lamb. One poem is addressed to Kirkstall Abbey, Leeds. It begins

> *Long years have passed since last I strayed,*
> *In boyhood, through thy roofless aisle,*
> *And watched the mists of eve o'ershade*
> *Day's latest, loveliest smile;*
> *And saw the bright, broad, moving moon*
> *Sail up the sapphire skies of June!*

And it ends

> *Adieu!—Be still to other hearts*
> *What thou wert long ago to mine;*
> *And when the blissful dream departs,*
> *Do thou a beacon shine,*
> *To guide the mourner through his tears*
> *To the blest scenes of happier years.*

Watts became a personal friend of Wordsworth, Coleridge and other literary figures. There is a letter from Wordsworth acknowledging the receipt of a *Leeds Intelligencer* 'containing a critique of my poetical character.' The poet's asperities lie beneath a garnish of courteous phrase but it is clear that he didn't think much of the literary critic concerned.

If Watts is remembered at all it is for a weird alliterative 'poem' in lines arranged alphabetically—

> *An Austrian army, artfully arrayed,*
> *Boldly by battery besieged Belgrade;*
> *Cossack commanders cannonading come,*
> *Dealing destruction's devastating doom—etc.*

But this is just a specimen of what can only be called his larking in letters. When he returned to London, he edited annuals and his repute is summed up in a couplet that went the rounds of London some years later:

> *Alaric A, weaver of 'New Year's Gifts', ingenious Watts,*
> *Of 'Souvenirs', 'Albums' and 'Forget-me-Nots.'*

Well, let us forget-him-not, and look indulgently on his rather magnificent posture. He once compiled a kind of *Who's Who*. It contained, of course, biographical details of famous and immortal Victorians—but few were given more space than Alaric A. Watts Esq.

In 1829 an amended partnership was established at Leeds. Robinson departed—among other things to assist Constables in publishing the Waverley novels—and Hernaman was joined by Robert Perring who edited the paper with notable distinction for the next dozen years. The war with the *Mercury* reached a new crescendo during this period. In response to some derisive comments by Baines on the dismal profits of the *Intelligencer* this admirable piece of rhetoric was printed

> As well might we say that the portly proprietor of the *Mercury*—the Sexagenarian dandy of Briggate—the Solon of the Leeds Workhouse—the Demosthenes of the Hunslet rabble—the father of Talbot Baines, Esq., the barrister-at-law—the sire of that *sola voluptas*, the travelled Adonis—and the lord of the manor of a piece of Lancashire moss . . . is still the same poverty-stricken adventurer that he was thirty years ago, when he wandered into Leeds, his whole fortune centred in a 'composing stick' and his head as empty of learning as his back was bare of clothes.

Nevertheless the *Mercury* at that time was a more influential paper than the *Intelligencer*, riding high on the tide of Liberal triumph. Watts and Perring between them did much to identify their Conservatism with the cause of the workers—so effectively indeed that they won over the friendship of Richard Oastler, the 'factory king', who abandoned Baines when he realised that in fact the Whigs were the friends of the mill-owners.

Under Perring the paper was conducted with boldness on other fronts. He defied the Leeds Town Council when they tried to stop publication of their proceedings, telling them that he would not tolerate any curb on the liberty of the Press. He introduced new techniques and new machinery.

But it was his successor, Christopher Kemplay, who, in a time of rapid change and swifter communications, gave the paper that stamp of 'Yorkshireness', that peculiar *sentiment*, which has typified it ever since. Kemplay was the son of a Leeds schoolmaster. He was educated at Ripon Grammar School and as a young man edited the *Yorkshire Gazette* at York. Changes in the proprietorship at Leeds, however, enabled him in 1848 to become the virtual owner-editor of the *Leeds Intelligencer*, and during the next quarter-century he was to lead it from being a localised weekly into a county daily.

Perring had been a keen controversialist; Kemplay was of a different stamp. He was less concerned with banging heads than with persuasion and enlightenment. He was himself something of a scientist as well as a man of letters; he exercised a wide-ranging intelligence and a zeal for improving the lot of his fellows. While he held high the banner of Conservatism against 'Whig jiggery-pokery', rejoicing in the recovery of Tory influence, his heart was really in social reform and the development of new 'scientific' amenities.

The terrible cholera epidemics stirred him to advocate better sanitation and more open spaces. He focused attention on overcrowding and backed a movement for 'model cottages' for the workers. His particular hobby-horse was smoke abatement; he looked with compassion on the lot of those who had to endure the filth and grime of the industrial West Riding.

While seeking always to produce 'a paper fit for a gentleman's table' Kemplay's *sentiment* enabled him to print also 'detailed reports of scandalous misconduct' and selections of 'miscellaneous items of the widest possible interest.'

Gradually during the early 1860s he began to prepare his readers for a great transformation and a wider circulation, and on July 2 1866, exactly 112 years after its foundation, the paper ceased to be a weekly and emerged as the daily *Yorkshire Post and Leeds Intelligencer*. At the same time Kemplay transferred his interest to a company called the Yorkshire Conservative Newspaper Co. Ltd. which, under the recently modified name of Yorkshire Post Newspapers Ltd., still operates it as part of the United Newspapers group. The paper continued to call itself the *Yorkshire Post and Leeds Intelligencer* until 1883 when, in response to popular usage, it became more simply the *Yorkshire Post*.

Meantime back in 1866 Christopher Kemplay sold off his old type, steam engine and printing press, announcing that the new directors had 'provided machinery that will suffice to provide a daily copy of the *Yorkshire Post and Leeds Intelligencer* to well-nigh every Parliamentary elector in the County of York.' The first Board of the new company numbered sixteen, the chairman being Mr William Beckett Denison of Beckett's Bank, Leeds (now part of the Westminster). He was a grandson of Sir John Beckett, the first baronet, of Meanwood Park, Leeds. Other directors included the Hon. George Lascelles, Viscount Nevill, and Mr John Musgrave Sagar-Musgrave—names intimately identified with the shire and the town.

Policy was re-enunciated in the first issue of the daily. It noted that opinions existed subversive of the social system; equally that defects were apparent in existing institutions. 'By these two guiding facts the political conduct of the *Yorkshire Post* will be regulated. It will be at once Conservative and progressive—a foe to democracy and revolution but the firm friend of all constitutional Reform.'

What howling demonstrations would be staged if any modern newspaper were to proclaim itself 'a foe to democracy'! As times change so do the meanings of words.

At the then handsome salary of £550 a year John Ralph was appointed editor. During his sixteen years in the chair he consolidated the paper, as one contemporary said, 'upon a level of excellence with the best daily papers in London.' He expanded the commercial news and the foreign correspondence and was a painful goad to North Country local councils for their failure to deal with stagnant drains and the 'filthy dwellings of the poor' which were the cause of so much pestilence.

In 1882 Ralph was succeeded by Charles Pebody, a sensitive

writer and journalist, full of original thought and sparkle. He
was something of a theologian and took a sharp interest in the
Anglican Church, but he is chiefly remembered wherever printers
foregather for his notorious handwriting. Eight to ten—or
sometimes as much as a dozen—words were feverishly scrawled
across each sheet of copy-paper; these were thrown on the floor
to be collected every few minutes by a boy and rushed to one of
the only two compositors in the building who knew how to read
what was written on them. Examples of this celebrated calligraphy
are reproduced on this page.

Pebody died in 1890 and was followed by Henry John Palmer,
less of a writer but more of an editor. A contemporary said
that he was 'for ever improving his paper. He flung aside the
worn-out garments of a jaded journalism and dressed up his
columns in the fashion of the day, but always with this proviso,
that they remained seemly.' He was jealous of the good name of
his craft. Journalism, he declared, 'always had, and always

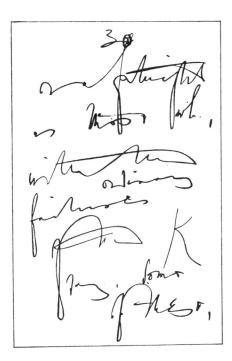

The handwriting of Editor Charles Pebody

Ladysmith Relieved—A *Yorkshire Evening Post* bill, February 28, 1900

will have, what the clergy sometimes call 'a preaching order'.'
Palmer saw some good in the birth of the Independent Labour
Party under Keir Hardie and some evil in the Church. The poverty
of the clergy, said his paper, 'is no shame to those who endure it;
it is a shame to the wealthier members of the Church of England.'

When, at the early age of 49, Palmer died, his chief leader-
writer, J. S. R. Phillips was appointed in his stead. Palmer
had been rather austere; Phillips was warm-hearted, genial,
humorous, immensely popular with his staff. He was a 'writing
editor', of a school that has now almost disappeared, and he
wielded a pen that could be gracious as well as barbed. The
Yorkshire Post became even more renowned as a journal of opinion. Phillips was fortunate in having as chairman of the Company

Lord Faber, a man of similar temperament, and between the two there developed a close friendship.

It fell to J. S. R. Phillips to pilot the paper through the turmoil of the first World War: he did so with consummate skill and balance, developing a wide range of what we now call 'background news' about the tremendous events of the time. Both he and Lord Faber died within a year, and during 1919-20 the *Yorkshire Post* acquired one of its most notable chairmen and one of its most distinguished editors. The Hon. Rupert Beckett succeeded Faber and Arthur Mann succeeded Phillips.

Rupert Beckett was the kind of being who comes to mind when one attempts to realise an embodiment of 'Yorkshire.' Stoutly-framed, florid, plain-spoken, he was outwardly gruff; yet he harboured his share of Sterne's *sentiment*, for if he inspired a certain dislike among a few for whom he had but an indifferent opinion, there are plenty of others who remember him for generous impulse, quick sympathy and gentleness. Rupert Beckett could be irascible. He had his gloomy moods when a favourite expression was, 'Bankers ain't rich, you know', but it is untrue, as legend affirms, that he never smiled. Although his banking interests occupied much attention it was the *Yorkshire Post* in which he took most pride. He knew it was a great newspaper and he was jealous of its reputation.

Arthur Mann, as one remembers him in the 'twenties and 'thirties, was a strangely *cool*, detached, aloof character, given to few words. He was shy and avoided social activity. People said he was 'stand-offish'; they had yet to learn what a formidable resolution lay within his quietude. He gave up the editorship of the London *Evening Standard* in order to gain that of the *Yorkshire Post*, and that is a measure of the esteem he had for the paper.

Despite his revulsion for 'popular' journalism, Mann moved the *Yorkshire Post* into 'seemly' changes in typography and modernity and introduced new features; but it is for his influence on two historic crises that he and his paper are remembered. He lighted the fuse which exploded in the abdication and, against violent opposition, particularly from Conservatives, he fought Chamberlain's appeasement policy to the bitter end.

On December 1 1936 the Bishop of Bradford, Dr Blunt, made significant reference to the pending Coronation ceremony and

A Daimler distributing miniature copies of the *Yorkshire Post* at the beginning of the century

the King's duty as a Christian monarch. Fleet Street realised the pertinence of this speech; the King's friendship for Mrs Simpson was well-known; but Fleet Street remained silent. Not so the *Yorkshire Post*. In a leading article the following day it said:

Most people by this time are aware that a great deal of rumour regarding the King has been published of late in the more sensational American newspapers. It is proper to treat with contempt mere gossip . . . But certain statements which have appeared in reputable United States journals, and even, we believe, in some

Dominion newspapers, cannot be treated with quite so much indifference. They are too circumstantial and have plainly a foundation in fact. For this reason an increasing number of responsible people is led to fear lest the King may not yet have perceived how complete in our day must be that self-dedication of which Dr Blunt spoke if the Coronation is to bring a blessing to all the peoples of the Empire and is not, on the contrary, to prove a stumbling block.

The fat was in the fire. Fleet Street had something to follow and *The Times* was able to quote the *Yorkshire Post* in making further comment the next day.

During the same period it was foreign policy to which the *Yorkshire Post* devoted increasingly outspoken attention. It was the era of disarmament, peace above everything; it was also the era of Nazi emergence and Hitlerian shrieks. The *Yorkshire Post* was not deceived as many others were. In resolute fashion and despite the criticism of readers and politicians, it set its face against the trend of the time—a trend in which the Conservative Party as well as the Socialists was involved. Leading article after leading article criticised national folly and stressed the national danger.

In November 1936 the Conservative Prime Minister, Stanley Baldwin, confessed to the Commons that he could not undertake rearmament because the prevailing pacifism of public opinion would not have it. The *Yorkshire Post* conceded that a policy of rearmament might indeed mean the return of a Socialist government committed more thoroughly to neglect of the country's defences, but, it continued,

> Even when political defeat is probable, still it cannot be the duty of the country's elected leaders to keep silence on matters vital to the very existence of the nation and Empire. The consequences of their meek submission to ignorant popular sentiment may be infinitely more grave than would be temporary defeat of themselves and their programme.

Little imagination is needed to see what dismay this caused at Westminster and what anger it aroused in Conservatives who blandly assumed that the *Yorkshire Post* could be relied on to toe

Yorkshire Post mastheads of 1940 and 1974

the Party line. But Winston Churchill read it with relish. As he must have done the subsequent opposition of the paper to every stage of appeasement. Neville Chamberlain was treated with courtesy as a man caught in a cleft stick, but also as a man under the spell of delusion. Arthur Mann had a clear eye fixed on Hitler and the roaring blast-furnaces of Germany. In one editorial the *Yorkshire Post* said, 'Our aim throughout has been to contribute to national unity and strength. To keep silence on causes of dissension and distrust cannot further this aim, and would be nothing less than a failure in patriotic duty.'

Unpalatable truth is never popular and the sales of the *Yorkshire Post* during this period had fallen to around 30,000 copies a day. In February 1939 critical voices were raised at the annual meeting. Rupert Beckett told Arthur Mann's opponents, 'In so far as you ask me to say anything which will tie the hands of this newspaper and prevent it from giving free and honest expression of its view on policy which may be vital to this country, I shall not sit here and consent to that.'

War, when it came, brought an acute problem. For some years the Yorkshire Conservative Newspaper Co. had owned its old

The *Yorkshire Post* building in Leeds

97

Prince Charles at the official opening of the *Yorkshire Post* Newspapers new Headquarters in Leeds, December 1970. Extreme right Mr Bill Bowes, ex-Yorkshire and England cricketer. On his right, Mr Gordon Linacre, Managing Director, Yorkshire Post Newspapers

rival, the *Leeds Mercury*. The *Mercury* flourished in the manner of popular journalism. It was crisp, breezy and picturesque. It sold some 100,000 copies a day to the less sophisticated populace of Leeds and district. It was admirably edited by Mr W. L. Andrews, later Sir Linton Andrews. But under wartime conditions could both papers remain viable, especially with the small circulation of the *Post*? After careful investigation a committee of the board which included Mr Colin Forbes Adam, decided they could not. The two papers ought to be merged as the *Yorkshire Post and Leeds Mercury*. Arthur Mann was totally and vehemently opposed to such a merger and he was also tired after some years of anxious stress. He resigned, and Mr Andrews was appointed editor of the combined paper.

To marry the popular *Mercury* with the 'quality' *Yorkshire*

Post was a difficult, almost an impossible, task, and there is small doubt that for a few years the *Post* lost prestige, though it acquired a surprisingly large part of the *Mercury's* sale. Andrews had been given an onerous job—to try to hold the readers of two fundamentally different publications—but in the end, by gradually allowing the *Mercury* characteristics to fade away and restoring the *Post* to its appropriate 'quality', he succeeded.

Sir Linton continued as editor until 1960, when he was well into his seventies. He had served the company with distinction in the chair of both its dailies for some forty years. He became an eminent figure throughout Yorkshire and within the profession of journalism, being one of the earliest chairmen of the Press Council: he was always a stalwart defender of the Press against

Sir Kenneth Parkinson, Chairman of Yorkshire Post Newspapers, with Prince Richard of Gloucester who toured the new *Yorkshire Post* building

The editorial hall in the new Yorkshire Post Newspapers building

uninformed criticism. In his active years he was a man of rapid decision and unfailing courage, and he carried all his responsibilities with enviable ease. His autobiography, published in 1964, takes the reader back to reporting days in Hull, Sheffield and Huddersfield at the start of the century and contains many fascinating stories.

After his retirement Mr Kenneth Young edited the paper for a brief period, adding to its literary repute, and was followed by Mr Edward Crossley who had been news-editor under Andrews. Crossley was an accomplished journalist, an effective writer and a witty and trusty friend. The whole staff had an affection for 'Ted' and his untimely death in 1968 was a blow to the paper. He was succeeded by Mr John Edwards, the present editor, under whose direction the *Yorkshire Post*, dressed anew though still in 'seemly' style, is determined to maintain its traditions.

This account has followed its fortunes largely in the persons of its editors. Many others of course—directors, managers and craftsmen—have contributed to the progress of the company, and a conclusion to this brief survey is fittingly provided by the latest and greatest business development associated with the *Yorkshire Post*.

From its first appearance as a daily in 1866 it was published at Change Court, Albion Street, Leeds. The premises were rambling and, despite many extensions and adaptations, became increasingly inconvenient. After a hundred years of service it was realised that they could not enable the *Yorkshire Post* and *Evening Post* to keep abreast of modern demands. Under the chairmanship of Mr Forbes Adam, whose period at the head of the company brought resolution on many important issues, the board decided to build and equip the finest possible newspaper office that brains could conceive and money could buy.

Today the *Yorkshire Post* and its companion evening paper—of which more will be told—are produced at Wellington Street. The great building, formally opened on December 10 1970 by the Prince of Wales, is of striking modern design and within it function the most sophisticated newspaper machinery and instrumentation in Europe. Some five million pounds has been invested in this enterprise which draws newspaper 'pilgrims' from all over the world, eager to inspect 'the *Yorkshire Post* at Leeds.'

SHEFFIELD'S *TELEGRAPH*

Hail to the Lord's Anointed,
Great David's greater Son;
Hail in the time appointed,
His reign on earth begun!

ASK any Sheffield journalist about the birth of his craft in the city and he will immediately refer to the author of this hymn, James Montgomery. For Montgomery founded a paper called the *Iris* in 1794 which, by its outspokenness and literary quality, focused national attention on Sheffield and its Press. The *Iris* was not the first paper to be published there. The *Sheffield Weekly Journal*, later the *Register*, had been started in 1754. This however was absorbed by the *Iris* at its foundation.

Montgomery stands rightly as the father figure of Sheffield journalism, and he may be said to have stamped something of his character on the city's later newspapers. Sheffield has long had a reputation for what is called 'campaigning journalism'—a reputation that never stood higher than it does today—and James Montgomery was above everything else a campaigner—in his hymns and poems a campaigner for Christianity and in his newspaper columns for social reform and individual liberty. The remaining lines of the verse just quoted testify to the spirit that animated him:

He comes to break oppression,
To let the captive free;
To take away transgression
And rule in equity.

Some other lines which he printed during the post-Revolution period when Britain was at war with France landed him in jail for publishing a seditious libel. They had been composed by 'a clergyman of Belfast':

> England's fate on the contest's decision depends,
> Most important its issue will be;
> For should France be subdu'd Europe's liberty ends,
> If she triumphs—the world will be free.

Montgomery's trial was extensively reported, with commentatory touches. We read that Mr Tooker, for the Crown, 'in a very able and learned speech, pointed out the excellence of our glorious constitution', while Mr Vaughn, for the defence, 'made the most eloquent, ingenious and animated speech we recollect ever to have heard in this court'—the West Riding Sessions at Doncaster. That ingenious speech, however, did not save Mr Vaughn's client from being committed to 'The Castle of York' for three months.

If the *Sheffield Daily Telegraph* cannot lay claim to have emerged out of Montgomery's *Iris* it may claim to have been started in order to fill the vacuum created when the *Iris* ceased publication, for it first appeared in 1855, the year after Montgomery's death. Moreover it appeared straight away as a daily, printed at 8 a.m. This was eleven years before the *Yorkshire Post* transformed itself from a weekly into a daily and places the *Telegraph* among the first of its kind.

From the start it was priced at one penny and for much of its life it was to declare proudly its reputation as 'the oldest penny morning paper in Great Britain.' Maybe this keen sense of economics and the appeal of 'value for money' stemmed from the circumstance that it was founded and edited by a Scot. His name was Benson, his initial was G., but for the rest practically nothing is known of him. Where he came from, whither he went, nobody knows and the swiftness of his departure plus the manner of his initial marketing leave a faint suspicion in the mind of the beholder. One of his employees later described how Mr Benson set about his enterprise:

> He provided himself with a map of the town and, among other details, noted the localities where men who had nothing to do could be found. From these he made a selection and employed them to distribute his circulars. They were a powerful unwashed troop in the

rough, elected mainly for their bold, persuasive style of address, but they met their employer well washed and shaven.

To each man he gave the requisite number of circulars for a certain district. These papers were to be delivered, and the replies (with cash) collected at another specified time. Upon the due fulfilment of these instructions depended the remuneration of the brigade, and so well was the whole process contrived that the employer managed to overlook all the men personally at their work.

He was within sight and call of every messenger, who had to report progress to him every half-hour.

In vulgar parlance, there were no flies on Mr Benson. His system appears to have been: get your orders, collect the money in advance, then print your paper. Maybe not a few Sheffield householders, confronted by a character with a 'bold, persuasive style of address' on the doorstep, felt that a subscription was the lesser of two possible evils.

At any rate Benson managed to get the *Sheffield Daily Telegraph* through ten days of existence. Then he vanished from all known record; one cannot help wondering whether any subscriptions went with him. If they did, the man who had published the paper for him was not unduly concerned; he felt that Benson had been on to a good thing and continued to produce the *Telegraph* on his own account. He was Mr J. Pearce, a printer of Aldine Court.

Pearce was a scholarly man, devoted to books, music and pictures and after three years he grew tired of editing the *Telegraph;* the daily demands on his time irked him; so he appointed Mr W. Shepherdson to the chair. But even the role of comparatively easeful proprietor was not to provide Pearce with enduring satisfaction. For more than thirty years there had been in existence a weekly newspaper called the *Sheffield Independent*, first produced from the unprepossessing address of 'Snig Lane.' Around 1862 it became known that the *Independent* was going to turn itself into a daily and Pearce was dismayed by the prospect of having to face the rigours of daily competition.

Among his contributors was a London barrister named

Frederick Clifford. Pearce had much regard for Clifford and consulted him about the possibility of selling the *Sheffield Daily Telegraph*. Clifford got in touch with a friend, William Leng, of the Scottish publishing family who owned the *Dundee Advertiser*, and on January 1 1863 the two of them bought the *Telegraph*, at once relieving Pearce of his anxieties and bringing to the paper a skill and dynamism which were to establish it as one of the leading journals in the country.

The new proprietors styled themselves Leng, Shepherdson & Co., the 'Co.' referring to Clifford who chose to remain in the background, possibly because he was working for *The Times*. Shepherdson was the man who had edited the paper under Pearce. He now became manager of the business while William Leng assumed the editorship—a most distinguished editorship which was rewarded with a knighthood in 1885 and ended only with his death in 1902.

In one sense Leng was fortunate from the start. Big news was abroad. The American Civil War was nearing a decision and the Sheffield public, like so many in England, were intensely interested in the fate of the Confederates. Leng tried to change their sympathies, and his arguments, while running counter to the popular tide, nevertheless drew controversial attention to the *Sheffield Daily Telegraph*.

Within three months of his arrival there also fell into his lap one of the biggest stories in the history of Sheffield journalism, the great Sheffield flood which was caused by the bursting of the Bradfield Reservoir. Homes were washed away and more than two hundred people died. Leng himself took a hand in reporting the disaster, and then made sure that copies of the paper were sent to the London newspapers, all of which reproduced large sections of its reports with acknowledgement to the *Sheffield Daily Telegraph*.

Up to this time the paper had only published leading articles occasionally but Leng saw that there should be an insistent voice reflecting the views and commenting on the news of so important a city. Leaders, apposite and forceful, now appeared daily; they were quickly characterised by that 'campaigning' outlook which has become a tradition in Sheffield.

Of these campaigns one of the first, and certainly the most

dramatic, was Leng's brave assault on a sinister movement which became known as the Outrages. This was an attempt by thuggery to impose dictatorship on trades unionists in Sheffield. It reached appalling proportions, including murder. The strong-arm boss was one William Broadhead of the Saw Grinders' Union. The climax of his activities came on October 8 1866 when the poor home of a man who was in dispute with the union was blown up by two of Broadhead's hirelings using a can of gunpowder.

Leng went passionately into the fray. He aroused public anger, disclosed the criminals and their tactics, and demanded a clean-up of trade union methods in the city. More than once his life was threatened but that did not deter him. The police insisted on giving him protection and so tense did the situation become that callers entering the editor's office often found themselves looking down the barrel of a revolver.

But Leng won. A Royal Commission was appointed and completely justified all he had revealed and what he had advocated. This performance of a public duty brought great prestige to the *Sheffield Daily Telegraph*, and its circulation and advertising revenue rose to handsome proportions. Emboldened by success, Leng and his colleagues began another venture. It started as the *Sunday Telegraph* but was quickly changed to *Weekly Telegraph* and became in its noontide a unique fiction magazine which older people will remember with a certain nostalgia.

Something of its quality can be judged from the names of authors whose work appeared in its columns. They included Wilkie Collins, Robert Louis Stevenson, Sir Arthur Conan Doyle, Emile Zola, Sir H. Rider Haggard and the Baroness Orczy. The *Weekly Telegraph* continued to exist, though then published in Scotland, until 1951.

Meanwhile the *Sheffield Daily Telegraph* was engaged in competition with the other morning newspaper in the city, the *Sheffield Independent*. Various families had owned the *Independent* in its early years before it came into the hands of Sir Charles Starmer. It was conducted vigorously as a Liberal organ and enjoyed a high reputation, but it was not outstandingly successful in the commercial sense and in 1931 it was acquired by its opponent. The new proprietors enabled it to continue separate publication until 1938, when it was merged into the stronger *Telegraph*.

The old pigeon loft, which housed the birds that carried the news to the Sheffield newspapers at the beginning of the century, was preserved until 1960 when work on the present building started

Nevertheless the *Telegraph* has always retained something of the *Independent* and in 1969 was proud to celebrate its 150th birthday, for the paper that had been absorbed went further back into Sheffield's history than the paper that had absorbed it. In its earliest period the *Independent*, like other provincial journals, had carried a goodly quota of national news. Its first issue, in December 1819, printed a picturesque account of how the Prince Regent had opened Parliament: 'His Royal Highness entered the House in his usual state, dressed in a blue coat with gold lace and attired in his robes.' One can only conjecture what Prinny's 'usual state' consisted of—a portly perambulation?

The *Independent* was agile in spotting bizarre episodes, no matter how far from Sheffield they may have occurred. It reported a wedding in Wiltshire where the bride's son appeared at the nuptials 'in an entire state of nudity, absolutely without shirt, hat, breeches or shoes.' The ceremony had to be postponed until

Sub editors at work in Sheffield seventy years ago

the guests recovered from their horror.

Some examples of how the law was applied at the 1820 Quarter Sessions in the West Riding are calculated to raise modern eyebrows:

> Thomas Linley, for stealing one cotton shawl at Sheffield, the property of John Girdner—to be transported seven years.
>
> Thomas Heeley, for stealing two linen shirts at Nether Hallam, the property of George Siddal, to be imprisoned two calendar months and privately whipped.

The proprietors who merged the *Telegraph* and *Independent* were no longer the original families. Great changes had occurred. Sir William Leng had died at the beginning of the century and the business had then been formed into a private limited company, with Lengs and Cliffords directing it. The company continued until 1925, when Charles Clifford was the chairman, but in that year it was bought by Allied Newspapers Ltd., the extensive group controlled by Lord Camrose, which later became Kemsley Newspapers Ltd. Although uncertainty about the bene-

fits of group membership must have been voiced at the time, the
Sheffield papers—the evening *Star* had long been in existence—
then obtained access to modern services, such as picture trans-
mission, a nation-wide news network, the use of aircraft, and
other rapidly developing facilities.

In 1959 the Thomson Organisation took control of the Kemsley
group and one of the first things the new owners did was to ratify
and encourage a project which had long been intended and but
for the war would have been carried out. This was the rebuilding
of the premises in High Street. Before it could be completed,
however, the *Sheffield Telegraph* and its companion *The Star*
had been acquired by United Newspapers. They pressed on with
the work and in July 1967 the new 'front door' was opened. It is
in York Street, not in High Street, for the rebuilding process had

Sub editors at work in the Sheffield editorial room today

Members of the United Newspapers Andes expedition. On the left the leader, Joe Brown

in fact shifted the *Telegraph's* home slightly from its old location. It had gone, as it were, next door.

And so the familiar white facade of columns, clock and dome, ceased to symbolise newspapers to passing Sheffielders. The new frontage in York Street is simpler and less romantic, but the arrangement is more convenient and, like the whole of the building, is in tune with the changing patterns and demands of the modern newspaper industry.

Similar considerations led to a change in title. In 1966 the *Sheffield Telegraph* became the *Morning Telegraph*. This was to meet the requirements of readers who nowadays want a morning

Sheffield *Morning Telegraph*, 1974

newspaper concerned not only with national and international affairs plus the day-to-day events of the city of Sheffield but also the events in the region surrounding it—a region which embraces north Derbyshire and parts of Nottinghamshire and Lincolnshire besides south Yorkshire.

Many figures eminent in newspaper management have been associated with Sheffield, of whom the late John Goulden, C.B.E., was an outstanding example. He directed the *Telegraph* business for many years with energy and distinction and in his last phase was on the board of United Newspapers. Among editors of the *Telegraph* who, by their professional skill and through long periods in the chair, contributed substantially to its shape and bearing, one recalls Mr J. Oakley (1912-37) and Mr F. K. Gardiner (1937-55). Mr Gardiner still lives at Sheffield in retirement. He was succeeded by Mr W. "Bill" Lyth, as ingenious a newspaperman as one could wish to meet. In the later part of his career Lyth turned his talents to management, and Sheffield mechanical departments will long remember him for his imaginative contraptions and cunning labour-saving devices.

Between 1961 and 1964 the *Morning Telegraph* was edited with distinction by Mr David Hopkinson (now editor of the *Birmingham Mail*). He added to the paper's 'campaigning' reputation by bringing to light symptoms of malpractice within the Sheffield City Police which resulted in a public inquiry. Since 1969 the paper has developed under its present editor, Mr J. D. M. Hides.

III

5

THE EVENINGS

EVERY weekday approximately 700,000 copies of evening newspapers owned by United are bought by the people of some fifty busy cities and towns, and clusters of villages. They are printed at seven centres—Leeds, Sheffield, Preston, Blackpool, Northampton, Wigan and Doncaster—but each serves a population dwelling in the surrounding region beside that of its base.

During the 1880s and 1890s evening newspapers sprang up all over the country and that is the period in which most of those belonging to United Newspapers were established. They are all prosperous and provide the bulk of the company's revenue. The duty of an evening paper is different from that of a morning; it is highly regionalised or localised. While naturally reporting important national and foreign events, it concerns itself primarily with the affairs of its area and is read intensively within that area—from which also it derives a substantial income from advertisements.

In the past two decades the position of the provincial evening paper has been greatly strengthened, thanks to the far-sighted resolution of managers in general. There used to be two, and sometimes three, evenings competing with one another in the larger towns and cities. This was a healthy state of affairs until rocketing costs, the advent of television, and other factors turned it into a precarious one. As each paper sought to fight its opponent it found itself having to sustain an even heavier burden and the financial position of some of them became extremely difficult. The prospect of both papers in a given centre destroying themselves was a real one.

This danger has been averted by a process of rationalisation. Agreements for mergers were carried through. In some cases the weaker paper was closed down. Today there is no provincial city or town in England where more than one evening newspaper is published. Frankly, this is a form of local monopoly, but unless the industry had taken such steps some towns would have found themselves without an evening paper at all, with a loss to communal life and a shrinkage of media for information, comment and advertising that would have been nationally serious.

Nevertheless the disappearance of immediate competition has placed on the editors of evening papers a new and important duty; to keep their staffs 'on their toes' and, by energetic direction, to ensure the maintenance of that efficiency which competition formerly stimulated. The board of United are keenly aware of this obligation to the public.

Evening Post, LEEDS

'LATE BUFF POAST!'

There are still many veterans who remember Alexander Paterson when he was editor-in-chief of the numerous papers published at Withy Grove, Manchester—'Pat' of the abrupt speech, wearing a black silk jacket, his bald head shining palely, like a twilit moon, along the dusty corridor. But long before then he had been the first editor of the *Yorkshire Evening Post* which originally puffed itself off its steam press on September 1 1890. He introduced it with the words: 'The prompt and accurate publication of news—news of all kinds—is the main business of the *Yorkshire Evening Post*.' His ninth successor, Malcolm Barker, takes the same words for his touchstone today.

The *Evening Post* is one of the world's most successful evening papers, though it had to struggle in its early days. It won its way by faith, determination and expert journalism. At the start of the Edwardian era it had six broadsheet pages, selling at the original price of one halfpenny. It strove to serve the county like its morning companion, but its strength has always been Leeds and the bustling towns immediately around.

Two elements have been consistent in the life of the *Evening Post;* an acknowledgment of 'extra-mural' duty on behalf of its population and a 'family' loyalty among its staff. In the mag-

A 'Buff edition' *Evening Post* masthead

nificent premises it now shares with the *Yorkshire Post* there
is a fine restaurant for the 'family' but in the old days there had
to be makeshifts, including that of Thomas Tweeddale, the stereo
overseer, who boiled soup on his furnace and sold it to everybody,
from the editor down to the dirtiest printer's devil. He com-
plained that he never made a profit, which is not surprising
since he teemed out a pint for a penny.

From its youthful years the *Evening Post* has been well aware
of the variegated life around it and the needs of many people.
The first part of this century saw much poverty and suffering
in the West Riding. In 1911 the paper organised a fund to provide
boots and stockings for the poor, and in the period between the
wars its 'Boots for the Bairns' campaign raised a total of
£98,688. Even today the editor receives letters from elderly
readers telling him that it was thanks to the *Evening Post* that
they had warmly-shod feet when they were children. The need
changes but the tradition persists. The paper now operates a fund
for old people, and during Ewart Clay's recent editorship it
raised £7,000 in order to distribute buzzer alarms to lonely
pensioners in the city.

A sharp eye for talent on the part of its editors has been an
important factor in the *Evening Post's* success. One of Paterson's
recruits was A. W. Pullin who, as 'Old Ebor', became surely the
most prolific, and certainly one of the most celebrated, cricket
correspondents in the land. For some thirty years his work
appeared in both the *Evening Post* and the *Yorkshire Post*, and
when death came to him in 1933 he was on a London bus heading
for Lord's to report a Test Match.

During the greater part of its existance the *Evening Post* had
the invaluable spur of fierce competition from the *Yorkshire
Evening News*. With tireless zeal the two papers pounded the
same beat and, in the process, pounded one another. There were
moments of high tension. Once the *News* accused the *Post* of an
'astounding suppression'. So far as one can now make out it

happened to concern not a suppression but a disclosure. However, confusion arises in all sanguinary encounters, and Leeds journalism looks back with some nostalgia on those 'battles long ago.'

For many years the *Evening Post* was printed on buff-coloured paper and strangers to Leeds were puzzled when they heard the street sellers bawling their singular anthem: 'Late Buff! Late Buff! All aht fer Yorksheer! Late Buff Poast!' But through periods of buff and white alike the paper has been fortunate in a succession of editors who knew their public and earned its trust.

Alexander Paterson was followed by Alfred Turner, who afterwards became editor of the London *Evening News*. Arthur Grime, of the Blackpool family, took over from Turner in 1911, later being appointed manager of the company. Robert Whittaker, an accomplished writer, edited the paper from 1923 to 1930 and Henry Futrell (a gimlet-eyed scrutineer of proofs) occupied the chair for sixteen years, until 1946. Then came Barry Horniblow from Fleet Street. He certainly galvanised the paper to a new circulation peak but his alleged partiality for 'hiring and firing' led to a rumpus, and he departed. By way of contrast there followed Alan Woodward, a large, reassuring, gentle man who injected his own sort of gumption into the columns.

When the *Yorkshire Evening News* was acquired and ceased publication in 1963 several of its editorial men were welcomed to the *Post* staff where they have more than made good with their old rival. The editor who was called on to tackle the problems

Yorkshire *Evening Post*, 1974

left by this swift disappearance of the *News*, including the necessity for extra drive, was Ewart Clay. Later, he also saw through the transfer of the *Evening Post's* editorial activities from Albion Street to Wellington Street. To everybody's regret Clay decided to retire early and left the company in 1970.

His successor, Malcolm Barker, inherited a highly competent staff and a plant capable of providing for a new era. Colour was introduced in 1971, and on October 15 that year, aided by the web-offset facilities, the first 40-page *Evening Post* was published, a fine augury for the days to come.

The Star, SHEFFIELD
REPORTING BY 'WIRELESS'

As a *news*paper, packed with items of direct interest to its readers, *The Star*, Sheffield, is a noteworthy example; but it is also outstanding for the manner in which it exerts vigorous editorial leadership on the life of a city that has won renown in recent years for its enterprise.

Its young editor, Colin Brannigan, was awarded the prize 'Campaigning Journalist of the Year' in 1971 for investigating and reporting on the condition of the needy in Sheffield. The operation involved inquiry into some 2,000 cases and resulted in a valuable social document which was published as a Penguin, *On Our Conscience*, written by Jack Shaw, one of the five *Star* reporters who worked full-time on the problem through 1970.

A year or two earlier *The Star* had been in the news for another notable achievement. This was the creation of what came to be known as the '44 Group', a gathering-together of local authorities and interests in the region surrounding Sheffield with the object of overcoming mutual rivalry and pooling ideas and endeavours for the general good. It was only after a long and painstaking campaign that the '44 Group' came into being. Len Doherty, the chief feature-writer of *The Star*, led and planned the exercise with unbounded enthusiasm and skill.

These campaigns were in accord with the paper's earliest traditions. It has never been politically tied in any Party sense and since its foundation it has identified itself with the well-being of all its people.

It started life on June 7 1887 as the *Sheffield Evening Telegraph*,

Front pages of the Sheffield *Star*, 1939 and 1970

the offspring of the *Sheffield Daily Telegraph*, The difference in personality between the two papers, evident today, was present at its beginning. The morning paper was a serious, measured 'organ' which spoke in columns of unbroken type, but the evening paper's editor, Alexander Lennox, wrote in his first issue:

> This journal is intended to be in the fullest sense a newspaper. In its columns the newest news will have precedence over everything else. Long reports, long articles and long letters will be conspicuous by their absence.
>
> In the interests of variety and vivacity there will, as at a well-ordered *table d'hote*, be a little of everything and not too much of anything.

There was a brief war between the *Evening Telegraph* and its only city rival, the *Evening Star*, a new venture by Joseph Cook and John Derry, the then owners of the *Sheffield Independent;* but this did not last, and within a year the *Telegraph* had swallowed its competitor and was publishing under the joint title of *Sheffield Evening Telegraph and Star*. However circulation expanded rapidly into a wider area and ten years later it had begun to call itself the *Yorkshire Telegraph and Star*.

There were several reasons for the paper's growth. As already

I

stated, it was non-political in a period when partisanship had become tiresome in the Press. It presented a very strong sports section. And in spite of Mr Lennox's original observation it called on its readers to share its life by encouraging letters to the editor. Even today there are few evening papers which devote so much space to readers' letters.

In 1920 the Starmer organisation in the city launched the *Sheffield Mail*. This led to intense battling which only ended eleven years later when the Lengs acquired the Starmer publications and the *Mail* was at once incorporated in *The Star*.

Another threat came during the same phase, this time from the first Lord Rothermere and his Northcliffe Newspapers. An *Evening World* was planned for Sheffield; a site where the Odeon Cinema now stands was secured, staff were engaged, and foundations for the building had actually been prepared when the truce was called which ended Rothermere's more ecstatic dreams. So *The Star* continued on its way unchallenged.

It was not afraid to try out new ideas, and the first use of 'wireless' as a reporting aid was made by *The Star* in 1922. Operators relayed to the office an address given at a meeting of the Sheffield Wireless Society so that a special edition could be printed and circulated to members of the Society before the meeting broke up.

During the late 1950s a change was made in format. For many years *The Star* had been produced as a tabloid but it was then re-styled in the page size now familiar throughout Sheffield and the region.

Among former editors are two men who occupy high position in the United group today. Mr J. G. S. Linacre, now managing director of Yorkshire Post Newspapers Ltd. and a member of the board of United, edited *The Star* from 1958 to 1962, and Mr T. P. Watson, now managing director of Sheffield Newspapers Ltd., the operating subsidiary, edited *The Star* from 1962 to 1968. Others who complete the roll of editors were R. E. A. Wright (1890-1910), H. L. Cooper (1910-38), E. R. Thomas (1938-42) and E. Gooseman (1942-58).

First issue of the *Preston Guardian*—the inscription reads 'The first impression of the paper taken at about 4 o'clock am 10 Febry—1844. J. Livesey'

Lancashire Evening Post, PRESTON

THE TALE OF THE TOULMINS

As with the Grimes of Blackpool and their *Gazette*, so at Preston the story of the *Lancashire Evening Post* is deeply involved with the Toulmin family. And the story really begins with the founding of the weekly *Preston Guardian* (now the *Farmers Guardian*) on February 10 1844.

The man who started the *Preston Guardian* was Joseph Livesey, a cheese factor, who achieved nation-wide celebrity as the 'father' of the total abstinence movement. He was a fiery zealot, proprietor of the *Moral Reformer* and similar anti-drinking publications, and when he decided to launch his weekly newspaper, mainly to fight the Corn Laws, he took as his chief assistant a young man who was one of the eleven sons of another cheese merchant. The young man was George Toulmin who had been born in a Preston cottage and had started work in a cotton mill when he was nine years old at a wage of two shillings for a 70-hour week. At fifteen he gave up cotton for printing, and in 1844 when he joined Livesey he had reached the position of printing overseer on the *Bolton Chronicle*.

George Toulmin, founder of the *Lancashire Evening Post*

George Toulmin was also an enthusiast for religion, politics and social work, and he and Livesey overcame all obstacles in establishing the *Preston Guardian* as a fine weekly newspaper which was read over a wide area of Lancashire. On October 15 1859 George, together with his brother James Toulmin took over the paper from Livesey, paying him £5,500 S.A.V. and presently other members of the family were brought into the business. They included George's youngest son, who later became Sir George Toulmin, Liberal M.P. for Bury and in 1909 chairman of the Press Association.

As the paper developed in circulation and repute the old premises in Cannon Street were abandoned for others at the present address in Fishergate. In 1882 the business became known as George Toulmin & Sons, proprietors of the *Preston Guardian* and the *Blackburn Times*, and four years later the *Lancashire Evening Post* was launched.

It was not the family's first attempt to enter evening journalism. Back in 1870 a go-ahead fellow called Anthony Hewitson had started a halfpenny evening paper, the *Preston Express*. A day or two afterwards, determined to have no nonsense from Mr Hewitson, George Toulmin began the *Preston Evening News*. But within three months both ventures died, and sixteen further years were to pass before Preston had an evening paper that was destined to endure.

Monday October 18 1886 saw the first copy of the *Lancashire Evening Post* come off the Toulmin press. It was old George's triumphal day. When he died, two years later, he had the satisfaction of knowing that it was well and truly on its way to abundant prosperity.

The paper has had a peculiar reversion of title. It began as the *Lancashire Evening Post* but in those days, when there was no national daily Press as we now understand the term, it was necessary to carry the morning's news and, indeed, to publish early morning editions. The Toulmins, ever sensitive to strict integrity in their dealings, felt that it was only honest to re-title their paper the *Lancashire Daily Post* and in 1893 that became its name. It was not until 1949 that it once more reverted to *Lancashire Evening Post*. Many older journalists still instinctively think of it as the 'L.D.P.' rather than as the 'L.E.P'.

One of the pony traps which delivered the papers in Preston before the first
world war

Lancashire Evening Post front pages of 1886 and 1974

For more than eighty years this newspaper has been one of the most influential 'voices' in the North West of England. Its story is one of steady growth and in the section about the *Evening Post and Chronicle* will be found an account of its penetration into south Lancashire.

Without any touch of sanctimoniousness it has remained true to the ideal originally set by George Toulmin—that social progress should be its aim and that this will not be accomplished if 'the motive power be one of hate and not of love.' There has never been anything bitter or cynical about the ways of the *Lancashire Evening Post:* it is held in the utmost regard by the people of its shire and is edited today with great ability by Mr Barry Askew who recently won a national newspaper industry award for drawing public attention to conditions at a Lancashire hospital.

Nor, despite its acquisition in the 1920s by William Harrison and its subsequent possession by United Newspapers, have the Toulmins ended their association. One remembers Mr G. F. Toulmin and Mr Maurice Toulmin, and today Mr Michael

Cynthia Bateman, *Lancashire Evening Post* writer, on jungle patrol with Lancashire troops in Malaysia

Toulmin is still with us, an expert in web-offset and other technical processes.

It is a peculiar characteristic of Lancashire journalism that it has always had an eye for 'poetry' and perhaps it is natural that Preston, the birthplace of Francis Thompson, should have made sure that poetic hopefuls were given an airing in the *Lancashire Evening Post*. Some of the Victorian efforts have a surprising crispness and daring, like this—

> *Providence sends the wicked wind*
> *That blows our skirts knee-high,*
> *But heaven is good and sends the dust*
> *That blows in the bad man's eye.*

West Lancashire Evening Gazette, BLACKPOOL
GRIME AFTER GRIME

Before you have completed a paragraph about Blackpool's *Evening Gazette* you feel you have somehow gotten yourself into the Old Testament. Not for a moment that there is anything antique in this extremely lively and efficient newspaper but because it is deeply involved in genealogy. It is folded around the Grime family as tensely as its reels of newsprint are rolled around its rotary presses.

For the story of the *Evening Gazette* is all part of the story of the Grimes. They began the business with the weekly *Blackpool Gazette* back in 1873 and fathers and sons, uncles and nephews, in a succession of accomplished and professional people, have been at it ever since. The business has prospered beyond its founder's sunniest dreams. So far as the Grimes are concerned there has never been the faintest symptom of 'clogs to clogs in three generations,' and even now, when United Newspapers Ltd. is the ultimate proprietor, it is still the Grime family that runs the *Gazette* and its associated publications with all its customary zeal. And that is a happy state of affairs.

Sir Harold Grime, an honoured figure in the British newspaper industry, formerly a chairman of the Press Association and a director of Reuters, is chairman of the company and editor-in-chief. The general manager is Mr John F. Grime, and until 1972 the editor of the *Evening Gazette* was Mr J. Favell Grime. He was succeeded by Mr F. B. V. Hargreaves.

Mastheads of the original *Blackpool Gazette* and the 1974 *Evening Gazette*

The early history of the business rightly belongs to that of the weekly paper and will be told in the next chapter. Here we are concerned only with the evening.

It was begun, after much family consultation, in 1929. The time appeared to be opportune for an evening paper in the bustling holiday town that had grown so sensationally in population and commerce. Actually the timing was bad, though nobody could have foreseen it. It was the eve of the dismal depression which hit Lancashire with particular force. Nevertheless the *Evening Gazette*, which had the temerity to launch itself on what is widely considered to be the unluckiest of days, May 13, was destined speedily to take a grip on life.

The family girded its loins and mobilised its strength. Mr Arthur Grime, who had been successfully managing the *Yorkshire Post* at Leeds, returned to Blackpool to lend a practised hand. 'Bert' and Harold were in executive charge. Harold had come back from Fleet Street where he was one of Northcliffe's bright sub-editors. He took over the editorship. Herbert, who was in due course to become president of the Newspaper Society, was already installed at home. Altogether they made a formidable team and it is not surprising that the paper won its way through every difficulty—and difficulties were plentiful.

By the outbreak of the second World War the *Gazette* was in a strong position, widely read not only in flourishing Blackpool itself but throughout the Fylde coast and its hinterland.

When the war came to an end the family process repeated itself. Alan Grime came back from the Far East, John (with a D.F.C.) from the Royal Air Force, and in due course Denis from the Fleet Air Arm. Arthur's son, John Favell, returned to Blackpool after working on the *Daily Express*—another example of acquired skill being devoted to the home enterprise. The Grime success is in large measure due to their constant invigoration by wide experience and a knowledge of up-to-date processes in Fleet Street and elsewhere.

In the 'forties and 'fifties the *Evening Gazette* continued to expand despite fearsome competition. It was never able to relax, to fall into flabbiness, for during the summer season it had to battle with as many as *thirteen* other evening papers. They came pouring into the town from places like Manchester, Liverpool,

Preston, Leeds and Bradford, and two were flown up daily from London—all eager to sell themselves to the hundreds of thousands of holidaymakers. In Sir Harold's words, it was a 'rugged free-for-all', but the *Gazette* matched the lot.

Times, however, were changing. Amalgamation and concentration were increasingly the vogue in commerce generally. How should the far-sighted directors of an important family business meet the situation? The question had cropped up before the Royal Commission on the Press in 1948. Herbert Grime and Harold Grime gave evidence. The chairman of the Commission asked them what they were going to do about death duties, to which Harold replied that they were too busy with the affairs of this world to worry overmuch about the next—a remark typical of a man whose humour has spiced more than one United dinner party.

The Commissioners smiled, but they had pinpointed a problem to which the Grimes were presently to pay serious attention. How they finally gained security in United without letting down a proud family inheritance has already been told.

Chronicle and Echo, NORTHAMPTON
FROM BRADLAUGH TO ROUSE

Nobody has a more intimate knowledge of journalism in Northampton than Mr L. W. Dickens, for long the editor of the *Mercury and Herald* and he has supplied this account.

The *Northampton Daily Echo* and the *Northampton Daily Chronicle* were started within a week of each other at the beginning of 1880, a year of bitter political rivalry in the town. At the General Election Gladstone became Prime Minister and at Northampton, then a two-seat constituency, two notable Liberals were returned. One was Henry Labouchere, the moderate, and the other was Charles Bradlaugh, the iconoclast, whose series of exclusions from the Commons after he had refused to take the Oath, and his repeated return at the by-elections which followed, made headline news in the two Northampton newspapers for several years.

Launched thus into stormy political waters, the *Chronicle* and the *Echo* stayed such keen rivals that for half a century any fraternisation between the staffs was frowned on. The *Chronicle* supported the Anglican Church and Conservatism, the *Echo*

Nonconformity and Liberalism, and there were many meetings to which only a reporter from the 'friendly' paper was admitted.

In 1931 when the two papers were merged, something puzzled the new proprietors, Provincial Newspapers. There came just then a remarkable bulge in circulation, but it had nothing to do with genius on high. The explanation was one of Northampton's most sensational events. In the early hours after bonfire night 1930 Alfred Arthur Rouse had burned the body of an unknown man in his petrol-drenched car on the outskirts of Northampton, where he was later tried and returned to Bedford Jail for hanging.

It was a new chief, W. Cowper Barrons, expert both on the editorial and business sides, who carried through the merger on the spot. At first there were problems of communication. Cowper Barrons was a Fifer and would talk, half to himself, half to sympathetic but baffled Sassenach members of the staff, with the added obstruction of a pipe clenched between his teeth. One day he gave the chief sub-editor certain instructions. 'Pardon?' said the chief sub. Cowper Barrons repeated his request. 'Pardon?' said the chief-sub. At the third 'Pardon?' Cowper Barrons said 'Never mind' and, walking to a desk, wrote down what he wished to convey. Unfortunately his handwriting was too difficult for the chief-sub to read.

Cowper Barrons had a rather parsimonious eye at close quarters but a wide and generous vision in the furtherance of good causes. During the war the *Chronicle and Echo* won the

Mastheads of the *Daily Echo* (20's) and the *Chronicle and Echo*, 1974

esteem of Northamptonians for its work on behalf of Service men and women and prisoners of war. Also during the war two of those celebrated entertainers, the Beverley sisters, were popular members of the staff—the twins Babs and Teddy. Babs worked in Cowper Barrons' secretariat, Teddy in the commercial department. They were so much alike that it was not until Teddy tried to pull instead of push a communicating door that Cowper Barrons realised she was 'standing in' for Babs while the latter had unofficial time off.

When the 1931 merger came both the *Chronicle* and the *Echo* were in shockingly cramped quarters and the *Echo* site was chosen for rebuilding. Today once again expansion and rebuilding are taking place. It was becoming increasingly obvious even when Mr Vincent Halton took charge of United's affairs in Northampton in 1958, that the town itself would have to grow or stagnate. Now it is destined to double its size as part of a great regional development which includes the creation of the new city of Milton Keynes.

During his fourteen years in Northampton as editor-in-chief and general manager Vincent Halton achieved outstanding success. There was a notable growth in the circulation of the *Chronicle and Echo*, especially in the breaking of new ground in North Buckinghamshire. Mr Halton cemented bonds of cordial goodwill between the Northampton readers and their newspapers and although he recently retired from executive work he remains on the local board and thus continues his association with the town. His successor as director and general manager is Mr W. Rogers, another old 'Withy Grove man', who faces formidable problems associated with the rebuilding operations. The *Chronicle and Echo*, now edited by Mr G. B. Freeman, stands at a peak of prosperity and at the threshold of great development.

Evening Post and Chronicle, WIGAN

DOWN IN THE LEAFY GLADE

Still they go on, making jokes about Wigan and its pier, and the notion has spread that of all the dreary smoke-pungent places in the country Wigan is the worst. It is utter nonsense, a baseless fabrication. If any of the jesters who have never seen the town

Brock Mill, a former calico printing works, the home of the *Evening Post and Chronicle*, Wigan. A river runs through the grounds

were to go to Wigan to visit the premises of the *Evening Post and Chronicle* they would be halted in astonishment. For it is the most picturesque and charmingly situated evening newspaper office to be found anywhere.

You leave the noisy main road and turn down a winding lane where ash, willow and sycamore sway beside a stream. Wild flowers abound, the throstle sings melodiously, bees bumble about the harebells. And in the green hollow of the clough you come upon Brock Mill where the *Post and Chronicle* is edited and published. Harley Drayton used to linger there, discoursing on the fauna and flora.

Brock Mill is a bit of Lancashire history. It stands properly beside its stream, a perfect representation of old textile days. It might have come straight out of Charlotte Bronte's *Shirley*. Now textiles have gone and United have transformed the mill into a modern newspaper centre. There are spacious editorial and management offices, a fine typesetting department and a lofty machinery hall.

How has this metamorphosis come about? The answer lies partly with Preston, partly with Manchester.

Preston, where the *Lancashire Evening Post* is published, lies to the north of the county, and some years ago, in order better to serve its southern area of circulation, it published an edition from cramped quarters at Wigan. Then came a change in the pattern of Manchester's evening press. The Manchester *Evening Chronicle*, having been taken over by its old competitor, the *Manchester Evening News*, was discontinued as a separate publication. It had always had a large sale to the west of Manchester, in towns like Wigan itself, Warrington, Atherton, Leigh, Adlington and St Helens. An arrangement was entered into between United and the proprietors of the *Manchester Evening News* whereby the *News* undertook not to exploit this area. The goodwill attached to the *Evening Chronicle's* title was disposed of to United and it was decided that the south Lancashire edition of the *Lancashire Evening Post* should become the *Evening Post and Chronicle*, based on Wigan.

The existing plant and premises were quite inadequate to meet the needs of the many *Evening Chronicle* readers thus acquired, and after pertinacious inquiry on the spot by Mr Barnetson—during which an old jam factory was seriously considered—the choice fell on Brock Mill. The interior was stripped and refashioned, new plant was installed, staff appointed, the approach road improved, and on 4 October 1965 the *Evening Post and Chronicle* was published there for the first time. The venture has been highly successful and today the paper has a strong and growing hold on southern Lancashire.

So in summertime the sub-editors, lino. operators and machine room staff picnic among the birds and flowers around Brock Mill when they take their snacks. The energetic editor, Mr M. Taylor, has not found this rural seduction a stumbling-block. On the contrary it refreshes his people. Maybe a few hawthorns in Fleet Street might provide inspiration.

Doncaster Evening Post
A SPRIGHTLY EIGHT-YEAR-OLD
Should you board one of the Pullmans that leave Kings Cross for the North around five o'clock in the evening you will prob-

Doncaster Evening Post ᴇᴘ

FURS, SHEEPSKINS, FUN FURS
Latest ranges now in stock
J. WINECOR
42 SILVER STREET, DONCASTER. Tel. 3152

Telephone Doncaster 4001   WEDNESDAY, SEPTEMBER 25, 1974   No. 2486   Price 5p

Town ᴇᴘ Edition

We specialise in PAINLESS EAR PIERCING
CHOICE SELECTION OF GOLD EARRINGS
GORDONS
JEWELLERS
3 & 5 Printing Office St., Doncaster.   Tel. 4198

The *Doncaster Evening Post*, 1974

ably be enjoying your dinner when the train slows down for the Doncaster points. As it then gains speed and dives under the North Bridge your attention will be captured on the western side by a large sign emblazoning the words *Doncaster Evening Post*.

How the *Doncaster Evening Post* came into being in 1966, as a cooperative effort between United Newspapers and Yorkshire Post Newspapers before they merged has been described. There may have been a touch of shoulder-glancing in those days; not now.

The paper is published in finely-equipped premises just beside the North Bridge. Its circulation has marched steadily since the beginning, although Doncaster has had to pass through a period of painful depression. The paper's success is due to its sheer excellence as an evening newspaper providing not only the news of Doncaster and the area between Tickhill and Askern but also expressing in this important industrial region an individual outlook upon the larger world.

It is alert in management and editorship, and there is something about the layout of the office which seems to symbolise this vigilance. When you go to see the general manager or the editor you walk along a corridor and gaze through side windows into the busy caseroom, and the effect is to make you say, 'Everything's brisk and above-board here.'

During its eight years of life the paper, like any other creature still in its formative youth, has had to meet with more than one wave of difficulties—more than one attack of growing pains—but it has met them in a spirit of counter-offensive. 'Wally' Moth, who has been in charge of the business since its inception, belies his name. He doesn't flutter; he thinks, then plumps. A familiarity with newspapers that began when he was a boy chasing along the passages at Withy Grove, Manchester, has given him the incisiveness that comes of wide experience. If there is anything about running a newspaper, or handling its prancings and

A party of readers from Doncaster went to Brussels on January 1, 1973, first day of Britain's membership of the E.E.C. Editors and senior executives of the company and their wives outside the E.E.C. Headquarters

The *Doncaster Evening Post* was launched on September 19, 1966. Here, the three Chairmen involved study the first issue of the paper. They are (left to right) Sir William Barnetson, Chairman, United Newspapers; Mr F. E. Hudson, Chairman, Doncaster Newspapers; and Sir Kenneth Parkinson, Chairman Yorkshire Post Newspapers

kickings, that 'Wally' doesn't know, it must be microscopic.

In his editor, David Evans, he has a colleague after his own heart. Between them they have brought a professionalism which bids fair for the future of the *Doncaster Evening Post*.

6

FROM COAST TO COAST

AN entwining of the Red Rose with the White into mutual
support and floriferous harmony—something which mortal eyes
have rarely, if ever, beheld since Henry of Lancaster and Edward
of York banged their bloody axes—this is what United has accomplished with its chain of weekly newspapers stretched across
Northern England. No such chain can be found elsewhere in this
country.

It begins on the seaboard of Lancashire and ends within a dozen
miles of the Yorkshire cliffs. Accept the truth that a few copies
of the *Beverley Guardian* find themselves in the houses of Hornsea
and Withernsea, and you realise that the chain runs all the way
from coast to coast. It is strongly linked, too, with the helpful
presence of big brothers on each side of the Pennines, at Preston
and Leeds.

The aggregate circulation of these papers totals some 270,000
copies a week. They and their readers reflect and represent every
aspect of English life and activity.

Some are published in industrial towns where the inhabitants
are employed in heavy and light engineering, including motor-
cars, coal mining, cotton and woollen spinning and weaving,
printing, tanning, electronics, shipping and shipbuilding, and a
host of other modern processes.

Some function in rural areas which together embrace the whole
range of agriculture—sheep on the high fells of the West;
poultry in the Fylde; cattle, milk and roots in the lower Dales
and the Vale of York; wheat, barley, oats and milling in the
broad acres of the East Riding. It would be hard to think of any

kind of occupation that is not followed by some readers of these United weeklies.

Here is a brief look at them and their stories, told in fleeting succession from West to East.

Blackpool Gazette and Herald

A TONIC FOR JOHN

In the previous chapter something of the saga of the Grimes of Blackpool has been sketched, but nothing was said there about the original Grime who, by starting the weekly *Blackpool Gazette*, initiated the business out of which ultimately emerged the *West Lancashire Evening Gazette*.

He was John Grime, a compositor on the *Preston Guardian*. He was, as they say in those parts, 'badly and out o' sorts' and, either by judgment of the apothecary or from family concern, it was deemed that a change of air was essential if he was ever to thrive. Blackpool, of course, was not far from Preston, and

The beginning of the Blackpool Tower. Alderman John Grime, founder of the *Gazette*, played a notable part in planning the tower. Picture by courtesy of Blackpool Central Library

The week's news roundup pages 2—3

Blackpool Herald

Incorporating the Gazette & Herald

Shows and TV in the Weekender supplement

No. 8258   Tel. Blackpool 25231. Want Ads 29111   FRIDAY, OCTOBER 4, 1974   Price 3p

FLEETWOOD CHRONICLE

No. 8258   FRIDAY, OCTOBER 4, 1974   Tel. FLEETWOOD 2406   Want Ads Blackpool 29111   Price 4p.

Thornton Cleveleys Times

Shows and TV in the Weekender supplement

No. 8193   Tel Cleveleys 2241. Want Ads Blackpool 29111   FRIDAY, OCTOBER 4, 1974   Price 3p

Lytham St Annes & Fylde EXPRESS

No. 4513   THURSDAY, OCTOBER 3, 1974   Tel. St Annes 724236 & Lytham 6238. Want Ads Blackpool 29111. Price 5p.

Poulton-le-Fylde News

Shows and TV in the Weekender supplement

No. 8258   Tel. Blackpool 25231. Want Ads 29111   FRIDAY, OCTOBER 4, 1974   Price 3p

Mastheads of the *Blackpool Herald* group

all Lancastrians had a proper estimate of its health-giving breezes. So in 1866 John Grime, aged 26, betook himself to Blackpool, and whether it was the ozone or not he managed to go on breathing vigorously there until his 78th year.

His father had been a prominent member of Preston Town Council and John inherited a taste for politics and municipal affairs. He was a printer; what more appropriate than that he should start a paper in Blackpool? He was not daunted by the existence of a bi-weekly, the *Blackpool Herald*, which traced its history back to 1843, but his first two attempts to establish a rival ended in failure.

137

Early days in aviation at Blackpool

Pertinacity however was one of his principal assets and at last, in 1873, his *Blackpool Gazette* managed to root itself. It set out to cater more effectively than the older competitor for the changing needs of the young township which in those days had a population of only 7,200, but it was never plain sailing and it was not until the first World War that the struggle could be said to have been decisively won. By then John's two sons, Fred and Percy, had brought more youthful energy to the business.

When old John died in 1917 he was an alderman, magistrate and Freeman of Blackpool. Soon afterwards the sons amalgamated the *Gazette* with its old opponent the *Herald*. In the late 1920s, the weekly *Blackpool Times* was acquired by Sir Charles Starmer, who had lately started an evening paper in Oxford. This was the red light. It was another reason why the *Evening Gazette*, against all advice from the pundits, appeared in May 1929. Four years later, the ailing *Times* was purchased by the *Gazette*. So ended the fierce battle for survival of the three local weeklies which had gone on for generations.

Nowadays the *Blackpool Gazette and Herald* continues to

flourish, appearing every Friday. It has also begotten a family of smaller weeklies which penetrate more deeply into the surrounding area—the *Fleetwood Chronicle*, *Lytham St Annes Express*, *Thornton-Cleveleys Times* and *Poulton-le-Fylde News*.

Blackpool has long been the playground for all sorts and conditions of men, and the files of the *Gazette* mirror a great gallimaufry. On October 19 1909 the first aviation meeting approved by the Aero Club was held there.

> A run along the ground for a few yards while the double-bladed propellor got up speed, then the great machine rose gracefully in the air . . . Farman did not rise high, for this was but a preliminary canter . . . The machine once or twice almost skimmed the ground, and then it rose again. This was flying . . .

At the other extreme, demonstrating the wide range of fare for which Blackpool is renowned, this appeared in September 1932:

> On the first floor (of the Golden Mile exhibition) is Mary Ann Bevan, who is the ugliest woman on earth— or so her publicity asserts—who for company has La Belle Eve, who is reputed to be at the other pole of creation. Beautiful and seductive she looks—on her posters.

Lancaster Guardian

THEY CALLED IN A GEOLOGIST

Ever since Shakespeare we have venerated old John of Gaunt, 'time-honoured Lancaster', for his farewell speech about

> This royal throne of kings, this sceptr'd isle,
> This earth of majesty, this seat of Mars,

and he may reasonably be regarded as having been a diehard Tory. Yet in the very shade of John of Gaunt's castle, on a November day in 1836, twelve business men of Lancaster met to oppose Toryism there. They passed a resolution, 'That in the opinion of this meeting it is highly desirable to establish a paper in Lancaster on Liberal principles, in order to convey sound political and local information and to disabuse the public mind.'

They felt the public mind needed to be disabused because, having knocked out an earlier Liberal paper, the Conservative *Lancaster Gazette* was enjoying a monopoly. So they founded the

Lancaster Guardian to be conducted 'after the manner of the *Manchester Guardian*' (which was then only sixteen years old). The first issue appeared on January 28 1837. Averting their gaze from the royalist Shakespeare, they took the roundhead Milton for their guide and printed a quotation from his works as their motto: 'Give me the liberty to know, to utter, and to argue freely according to my conscience.'

The *Lancaster Guardian* has exercised that liberty ever since, to the great benefit of its city and the northernmost acres of the county Palatine. It has always been an advocate of reform and a faithful recorder of local affairs.

A certain Anthony Milner was the first printer and publisher of the paper, and the first editor was George Catt from Kendal. On a 'Columbian press' they produced 200 copies an hour. The printers started at 5 a.m. on a Friday and kept the press going till 10 p.m., working turn and turn about. In the mid-1850s a machine invented by Mr Soulby of Ulverston was installed, but though it was the forerunner of the world-famous Wharfedale it was an indifferent prototype: it wasn't much good and didn't last long.

Front pages of the *Lancaster Guardian*, 1837 and 1974

For eighty years the Milner family owned and conducted the *Lancaster Guardian* although they were deserters from Yorkshire, having forsaken their native Swaledale. In 1919 the paper was acquired by Sir Charles Starmer whose business subsequently became the present Westminster Press group. They in turn sold it to Provincial Newspapers.

In its 138 years of life the *Lancaster Guardian* has had its share of excitement. To the understandable dismay of the staff the front of its premises fell down in 1898 when they were rebuilding the Nag's Head next door. Long before then there was the day when a compositor found a three-foot snake in a quoin drawer. It was surmised 'that some bird of prey, flying over with the reptile in its claws, had dropped it through the skylight.'

The office was in commotion. The proprietor and other hierarchs were summoned for consultation and, having observed the snake and its alarming characteristics as it wriggled about the premises, they fell into such confusion over the appropriate science that they called in a geologist. For some days one of the reporters went about with string tied tightly round the bottoms of his trousers lest the snake should crawl up his leg. Finally it turned out that an apprentice had been the 'bird of prey.' A fellside lad, he had picked up the snake, taken it to the office, and popped it into the quoin drawer to await events. Having had rather more fun than he had hoped for, he tracked it down and tossed it back to the hills again.

Ormskirk Advertiser

REPORTING TO UNCLE

A twelve-year-old boy from Lancaster found himself in Ormskirk one day during the year 1829. His name was Tom Hutton. He made his way to a turning off Aughton Street where a printing press and lending library functioned under the direction of Messrs Leak and Johnson. Mr William Leak was Tom Hutton's uncle and the lad had arrived to 'report for duty'—and incidentally to found a local newspaper dynasty that endured for well over a century.

Tom worked hard and long in the little printing office; as he grew up the business expanded under his impetus; he became a partner and his personal affairs prospered. In 1846 he married Miss

From the *Weekly Advertiser* 1853, a supplement to the *Weekly Advertiser*, and a 1974 *Ormskirk Advertiser*

Ellen Garth of Colne and seven years later fulfilled a long-cherished ambition by producing the first copy of the *Ormskirk Advertiser*.

Throughout its existence the paper has kept steadfastly to the course Tom Hutton set for it. He determined that it should be the honest friend and servant of the home-keeping people of rural west Lancashire, and so it is today. From the beginning it chose good company; the first issue was turned off a hand press which also printed a family Bible.

The *Ormskirk Advertiser* soon established itself in its community and in due course Tom Hutton's son William helped his father to introduce new methods. A rotary press took the place of the old flatbed, bigger premises in Church Street were acquired, and the paper flourished commercially as its reputation spread.

When Alderman William Leak Hutton died in 1928 he left the business to his son Harold and his ten daughters. Harold turned it into a private company and held the managing directorship until the 1950s, when he was succeeded by Mr John Prescott who retired in 1973. Mr Prescott initiated many changes, the most important of which was the adoption of photo-setting and web-offset printing. The first web-offset *Advertiser* appeared on August 29 1967 and the paper was thus geared to meet the needs of a rapidly expanding readership which includes the new overspill town of Skelmersdale.

In addition to the *Ormskirk Advertiser* there are also published the localised *Skelmersdale Advertiser*, and *Maghull and Aintree Advertiser*.

Morecambe Guardian
MR SMITH'S VISION
Mr Malcolm Smith was appointed editor of the *Lancaster Guardian* in 1919. He lifted his eyes not only to the inland hills but to the western sea where Morecambe fronted its swift tides. He told his directors that they ought to heed the development of Morecambe. It was only five or six miles away but it was a different kind of place altogether from Lancaster and needed special attention.

True, the locally-owned *Morecambe Visitor* was thriving, but there was room for another paper in a resort that was so rich in commercial prospect. Mr Smith's arguments prevailed. In 1920 the *Morecambe Guardian* was launched and its success has justified him. The paper is printed at Lancaster but from the first it has been edited in Morecambe and it has become a highly

The *Morecambe Guardian*, 1974

esteemed native of the town. The present editor, Mr R. C. Quick, is as enthusiastic about Morecambe and its potential as was the far-sighted Mr Smith.

Each year the *Morecambe Guardian* elects a 'citizen of the year' who is given a handsome plaque and a handsome personal present. The luncheon at which the award is made has become a popular event and among those who have handed it over are Lord Derby and Sir Alec Rose, the round-the-world yachtsman.

Chorley Guardian
THE LADY OF MARKET STREET

Young Septimus Fowler was a compositor on the *Chorley Standard*. In later life he wore a beard but in 1866 he was less hirsute, better shaped for speed and enterprise, and when he heard that a printer and stationer in the town was going elsewhere he seized his opportunity by seizing the business. Within a year or two he had founded the *Chorley Guardian*. The first issue came out on November 4 1871 and its first news column (all in one paragraph) was an account headed 'Mr Gladstone at Greenwich.'

The *Chorley Guardian*, therefore, is just over a hundred years old, a prosperous newspaper which is widely read for its responsible coverage of the news and affairs of this important—and growingly important—centre. Nobody knows Chorley, or the history and people of central Lancashire, better than its present editor, Mr George Birtill, and his readers know *that*.

When Septimus Fowler started his paper Chorley was a town of cotton and clogs and knockers-up, self-sufficient, independent. The *Guardian* addressed itself to this individualism as its contents make evident. The 1870s were within the years when 'town hall mania' swept the country and early in the *Guardian's* career came a helpful controversy about what sort of a new town hall they should build. (It was to replace one which carried ram's horns on its clock and was known as 'Th 'owd Tup.') There was a stage when the *Guardian* spoke of 'a portentious silence anent the whole project', while another editorial comment said there was 'not a plan in the whole lot' that would suffice.

Septimus had a wife who was journalistically efficient, like Mrs Sanderson of Doncaster. She ran the paper when he was away. A bespectacled kindly dame she became so considerable a figure

Chorley's new fire engine blows off steam in 1900—a *Chorley Guardian* picture

that they called her 'The Lady of Market Street.' Her two sons carried on the business after their father, and it was only in 1927, when the Chorley Guardian Co. Ltd. was formed, that the family connection ended.

Few old files convey a better sense of intensive local news-gathering than those of the *Chorley Guardian*. To its paper the town was, rightly, the hub of things. We read in detail about torchlight processions with insulting effigies of Kruger after the Boer War; of a new steam fire engine in 1900—its jet sent water 'higher than the town hall'; of tramways, bursting flywheels, new schools, factory extensions, mayors, town clerks—and this little paragraph hidden at the bottom of a column on December 5 1896:

From the *Chorley Guardian* masthead, 1974

The old wire works at Leyland is now being fitted up with machinery for the carrying out of the manufacture of motor carriages. New boilers have been put down.

That was the first whisper of mighty things to come. Today Chorley and its near neighbour Leyland stand amid vast industrial development which has led to the recent launching of the *Leyland Guardian* in the rapidly growing town where the world-renowned name 'Leyland' means something rather more impressive than motor carriages built by steam power.

Wigan Observer

MR WALL WON THE GIRL

There are not a few experienced judges who consider the *Wigan Observer* to be the handsomest newspaper published in Britain. If this is in considerable measure due to web-offset printing it is also due to the staff's admirable use of type and layout and reflects the highest honour on successive editors, Mr Fred Dove and Mr Jack Winstanley.

In its first year on web-offset the paper won a bronze plaque as the best designed weekly in the land, and it was hard lines that Mr Winstanley, then assistant editor, who had played a leading role in the transformation, was suffering from an ulcer when he received the award at a Savoy reception and had to be content with a couple of glasses of milk instead of champagne.

Beautiful colour work is a feature of the modern *Wigan Observer;* appropriately, therefore, a touch of colourful romance brightens the story of its foundation. Back in the 1840s a young journeyman printer from Wolverhampton, Thomas Wall, went to Wigan. There his gaze was caught and held by a charming titian-haired girl, and he decided to stay in the town and see if he might win her. He did; she became Mrs Wall. And in due season Mr Wall became an alderman of Wigan and the proprietor of its leading journal. He published the first edition of the *Wigan Observer*, as a monthly newspaper, in January 1853, when a man and a boy, slaving hard, were able to turn off 250 copies an hour.

Two years later, on the abolition of the Stamp Duty, it became a weekly.

Thomas Wall died in 1904, aged 88. His sons and grandsons directed the business and edited the paper, completing a family record of 113 years, and the link is not yet broken, for Mr J. B. Dakeyne, now general manager, married a daughter of the late Mr Ralph Wall, grandson of the founder.

The first editor who was not a Wall was Mr Thomas Meadows, he occupied the chair from 1932 until 1956. His was a remarkable career for he was originally a pitman and decided to try his hand at journalism when recovering from an accident at the coal face.

If there has been a long continuity in the breed at the helm of the paper there has been a similar continuity in its character. 'As we proceed', said the first issue, 'we shall acquire experience, and no exertion shall be spared to render our little publication worthy of general support.' That blend of modesty and determination has guided the *Wigan Observer* through all its days, and

The first issue (1853) and a 1974 front page of the *Wigan Observer*

Mr and Mrs Harley Drayton at the opening of the new *Wigan Observer* plant

the 'little publication' of 1853 has become a *must* to the inhabitants of the town and district. Today it goes into practically every house—handsome, virile, exhaustive in its news coverage, well-written and wise in comment.

In 1953 a fascimile of the front page of the first edition was printed to mark the paper's centenary. It included an advertisement for 'several excellent houses to let' in Lansdowne Terrace, Wigan. Alas! the advertisement brought a woman hotfoot to the office, desperately seeking a home a hundred years later. 'What are the houses like?' she inquired.

The decision to adopt web-offset was taken by the Wall proprietors just before the business was acquired by United Newspapers. It was a far-sighted decision and United pressed on with its fulfilment. The first offset paper was produced on January 28 1966 when the Mayor of Wigan and Harley Drayton were among the onlookers. It contained this announcement, echoing the same note of modesty that had accompanied its foundation:

> If today's copy of this newspaper looks neater, nicer, and better printed it is because it was printed on our fabulous new web-offset press which was christened with this issue. If today's copy of this newspaper does not look neater, nicer and better printed, it is because no one really knows how to run our fabulous new press yet.

But today they know very well how to handle their 'fabulous' press, as every copy of the *Wigan Observer* testifies.

Blackburn Times

ON TOP OF THE STABLE

'The want of an organ by the Liberal Party in Blackburn has been long felt.' With these words the *Blackburn Weekly Times* opened its prospectus in the first issue, on June 2 1855. Thereafter it proceeded to fill the want with an energy that ultimately extinguished the Tory *Blackburn Standard*.

A Mr Fred Nichols started the paper, having earlier tried his 'prentice hand on the *Darwen Examiner*. He produced his first copy over a stable in Lord Street. Although within a few years other proprietors came along—Mr Joseph Greenwood and Mr Ernest King—the paper continued to be firmly attached to Liberalism

Blackburn Times

Blackburn's Friday edition of the Lancashire Evening Post

54,954   FRIDAY, OCTOBER 4, 1974   8p

1974

and the Chapel, one of its editors being a Congregational minister with the prickly name of the Rev. Horrocks Cocks. This affinity however did not deprive it of an ubiquitous nose for news and news values. Its first illustration, in 1856, was a woodcut of Palmer the poisoner, and when that gentleman was hanged a few months later the printing machine worked 21 hours non-stop, 'turning out 7,000 copies.'

In 1866 the *Blackburn Times* (by then it had dropped the word *Weekly* from its title) was acquired by the Toulmins of Preston, and it continued to be conducted by the family until 1927 when it passed to Provincial Newspapers. They took a hand in all its operations. Before the era of the motor-car John Toulmin would drive over in whirlwind fashion from Preston on press days and his phaeton with its pair of foaming bays was a familiar sight in Corporation Street. Today, though retaining its independence as Blackburn's own weekly, recording every Friday the affairs of the town under the shrewd editorship of Mr A. L. Fryer, it maintains a close association with its old companion the *Lancashire Evening Post* at Preston. Modern printing techniques, modern design, and the enthusiasm of a youthful staff, have combined to lift the paper firmly into the seventies.

Recently came the retirement of one who had rendered long and devoted service to the paper and its general printing activities —Mr F. E. Green, the general manager. It is 40 years since Mr Green joined the staff. He recalls particularly some hectic weeks during the second World War when—the *Times* having appealed to its many overseas readers for gifts for the children of Blackburn —he found his office stacked with four tons of sweets and chocolates.

The *Blackburn Times* has always been conducted with a sharp appraisal of changing conditions and new techniques, but innovation was never hastily adopted. When the first zinc block was made and shown to John Toulmin he took it to Preston in order to talk things over with brother George and, despite perpetual prodding, they debated for six months before giving their consent to its use.

Editors, however, have not failed to produce prompt comment on the latest intelligence, whether it concerned the Crimean War —'the *pen* has failed, the *sword* must now accomplish the work', wrote the *Times*—or the introduction of daylight saving. Both in the style of its leading articles and the scope of its features the *Blackburn Times* inherits a genuine literary tradition. Samuel Smiles of *Self Help* was one of the earliest contributors and the paper did much in Victorian times to encourage Lancashire's aspiring poets. The first issue contained a half-column review of Longfellow's *Voices of the Night*, a rather flowery but nevertheless perceptive essay. Mr W. A. Abram, its editor for some twenty years until 1887, has been described as 'the most distinguished man of letters after John Morley that Blackburn has produced.'

The old tag, 'What Lancashire thinks today—', is justified once again in the *Blackburn Times* of 1855. Under the heading 'Local Affairs' appears this item:

> The Blackburn Commercial Association at a meeting held on Wednesday last, at the Old Bull Hotel, adopted a petition to the House of Commons in favour of the adoption of a decimal system of coinage . . .

Burnley Express and News

A FIERY FURNACE

Burnley is well-named. Somehow the town seems to burn with a sombre power beneath its neighbouring uplands of heather and ghyll. It has consumed a host of papers and periodicals so that when you read the list you almost hear them crackling into ashes. A friendly society first had a go in 1781 but Burnley was lambently unfriendly. Then came the *Cottager's Magazine* and in 1846 the *Burnley Bee*. The *Burnley Advertiser and Monthly Summary of Events* went the way of all combustibles. There have been the *Burnley Mentor*, which endured the heat for only 18 issues, the *Burnley Standard* (17 issues), *Burnley Mercury* (ten weeks), *Burnley Radical* (13 issues), *East Lancashire Radical* (23 issues) and *The Socialist* (two years). All were burnt up in a short time and he is temerarious who seeks to enter this persistent oven with a new sheet, hoping it will not be scorched.

Burnley has suffered only three papers to enjoy any length of life, and little by little it has reduced them to one—the one it has never singed but steadily preferred, the *Burnley Express*.

It first came out on December 8 1877, the venture of Mr George Frankland, who produced it at the Bull Street Printing and Binding Works, and it has continued to operate from the same, though frequently enlarged, premises ever since. The site has always been a focal point of communal life and perhaps that is why Burnley felt that the *Express* belonged to its heart. The Bull Field, from which the name of Bull Street and the Bull Hotel were taken, was where in distant times the farming fraternity kept their breeding bulls.

In the depressed days of 1929 Burnley football fans gather outside the *Burnley Express* office where the F.A. cup replay results were posted in the front window. The crowd dispersed in glum silence—Burnley having lost at Swindon

Burnley Express

No. 10.830   FRIDAY, OCTOBER 4th, 1974   and Burnley News   EST. 1852   MID-WEEK 7p.   WEEKEND 4p.

1974

In 1887 the *Burnley Express* began to publish twice a week on—yes—a web-printing press called a Foster-Hoe. Some years earlier it had absorbed the *Burnley Advertiser* and in the same period it was sold by Mr Frankland to Sir John Thursby, a Conservative Parliamentary candidate. He appointed as editor a local journalist, Mr Lawrence Brotherton, who in 1890 became sole proprietor. His sons followed him in the business.

Throughout its history there had been only one serious rival to the *Express* despite the efforts of many others. This was the *Burnley News*, founded in 1913 with support from the Toulmins of Preston to promote the Liberal cause. But in 1933, when Provincial took over, the *Burnley News* was merged in the older paper which, adopting the title *Burnley Express and News*, remained the sole and triumphant survivor of the stricken field. It appears twice weekly, on Tuesdays and Fridays.

In recently modernised premises with frontages in Bull Street and Manchester Road, the Burnley property is among United's more substantial possessions. The *Express and News*, ably edited by Mr D. K. Hall, has a 'saturation' sale in the town. There are few Burnley homes where it is not studied every Tuesday and Friday. Mr K. Nightingale, the director and general manager, also has the oversight of the *Nelson Leader*, the *Colne Times* and the *Clitheroe Advertiser and Times*.

Nelson Leader AND Colne Times
NEWS OR VIEWS?

From early years these two papers have been inextricably mingled, either as rivals or in co-operation, and both today are edited by Mr Noel Wild, the printing plant being at Burnley.

Germinal operations began in a back-kitchen at Mosley Street, Nelson, in 1881. There Mr Middleton Coulton pedalled away at a primitive printing machine, producing theatre handbills. But he was ambitious and did not see himself pedalling in a back-kitchen for the rest of his days. Friends who knew the man were not, therefore, surprised when in 1890, under the imprint of Coulton & Co. he began publication of the *Nelson Leader*. The

1974 mastheads of the Nelson and Colne papers

battle for circulation with various rivals was desperate, and when Coulton acquired his first linotype machine ten years later it had only reached 2,000 copies a week. Nevertheless it managed to outstrip the *Nelson Chronicle* and absorbed it, leaving in the end only one competitor, the *Colne and Nelson Times* which had been founded at Colne in 1874.

Different policies were pursued by the two rivals. The *Times*, when conducted by a local Liberal, Sir James Aitken, became heavily political. The *Leader* avoided Party entanglements, concentrating on chasing the news and getting the pictures. Inevitably it went ahead and in 1935 Sir James sold his flagging *Times* to the Coultons. Thereafter it discontinued its Nelson activities and became the *Colne Times*, leaving Nelson to the operations of the *Nelson Leader*.

For many years the papers had separate editors and editorial staffs although the two towns are only a couple of miles apart. In 1937 the Coultons invaded Yorkshire by starting a localised edition of the Colne paper, the *Barnoldswick and Earby Times*, thus 'mopping up' the immediate area.

Over a long period the *Nelson Leader* was edited by Mr Tom Morgan and the *Colne Times* by Mr Joe Sunter—men whose journalistic abilities were matched by their repute as active and honourable friends of their tightly-knit communities. Mr Morgan was chairman of the Nelson Cricket Club which, in the 'twenties and 'thirties, was surely the most famous league cricket club in the world. Its professionals included Ted McDonald, the Australian fast bowler, and Learie Constantine, the famous West Indian player who ultimately became a peer of the realm.

154

Clitheroe Advertiser and Times
MR PARKINSON'S LAW

Approaching Clitheroe by road you used to find yourself one minute in Lancashire and the next in Yorkshire, for the frontier—border is too mild a term—wriggled all over the place thereabout. But following local government reorganisation several former White Rose villages are now within Lancashire. Clitheroe itself is officially and vehemently Lancashire, home of the Asshetons who have been sending members of their Lancastrian family to Parliament since the days of Simon de Montfort.

The *Clitheroe Advertiser and Times* cannot claim such longevity in public service. It was first produced on February 28 1885 by Mr J. Cowgill, at 27 Castle Street. Three years later Mr R. Parkinson, in the Market Place, came out with the *Clitheroe Times and Low Moor, Whalley, Chatburn and Ribblesdale Observer*.

In his first editorial Mr Parkinson stated the facts of life as he perceived them. 'There is not a fortune behind our undertaking,' he said, 'and it should be noted that for our continuance we rely upon the recognition of our efforts—not a recognition that comes empty-handed but one that comes with something out of which salaries can be paid.' In similar vein Mr Cowgill had stressed upon the business men of Clitheroe that his paper could bring before the public 'at a small charge any special article they might have to offer.'

Thus both papers seem to have had their sights well-adjusted, but in the end they discovered that they could only attain their objective in collaboration, and on May 7 1920 they were merged under Cowgill control. Since 1963 the paper has been one of United's little properties, vigorously serving the interests of its neighbourhood. Mr George Cowgill, his grandson Mr George Bryan Cowgill, and several others have edited the *Clitheroe Advertiser and Times* over varying periods. Since 1970 Mr Raymond Mann has occupied the chair.

Modern housewives, looking into early issues, would find some surprising prices. In the late 1880s advertisements offered Scotch whisky at 2s 9d a bottle, bacon at 7d a pound, beer at 1s 6d a gallon. In 1900 a confectioner announced a Christmas club at sixpence a week for ten weeks. Members received an iced Christmas cake, a raspberry sandwich, half a pound of biscuits,

COUNTRY MUGS
by JOHN BUCK at

THEO'S

THEO WILSON and SONS LTD
4 and 7 York St. Clitheroe. Tel. 22688.

Clitheroe Advertiser
CLASSIFIED .... TEL. BURNLEY 22331
ADVERTISING ...... TEL. CLITHEROE 22323
EDITORIAL .... TEL. CLITHEROE 22324
and Times

THURSDAY, OCTOBER 3rd, 1974
No. 4507
Price 4p

CLOTHES OF QUALITY
Sports Jackets
Sports Trousers
Two-piece Suits
FRED READ & CO. LTD
3 MARKET PLACE, CLITHEROE
Telephone 22302

1974

six macaroons, six 'puff shells', a sponge cake, half a pound of mince meat, lemon cheese, six mince tarts and a quarter of a pound of tea; in addition 'one of the prettiest pictures that has ever been published', entitled *Life's Springtime*.

Not bad for five bob. (25 pence if you are not old enough.)

Dewsbury Reporter

THEY BURNT IT

Across the frontier, some thirty miles inside Yorkshire and beyond the heathery heights of the Bronte country, is an industrial area known as the Heavy Woollen District, where United have a cluster of weekly newspapers.

The Heavy Woollen District is renowned for cloth of stubborn fibre and there are apocryphal tales about the capacity of its mills to turn anything into wearable fabric; it used to be said that they could 'weave owt'. And if the cloth is tough so are the people; a tenacious race, endowed nevertheless with a sense of lugubrious, often mordaunt, humour. A Heavy Woollen funny story goes on for a long time, is told with sombre deliberation, and becomes more fully-flavoured and absurd as it proceeds.

But they know how to preach as well as to laugh, and although in recent years the area has become a home of clubs where world-famous pop stars appear regularly, it is still the Chapel that commands its mind and shapes its outlook. The banner of Liberalism is staunchly upheld and several well-known Liberal politicians were born and bred there.

Dewsbury is the capital of the Heavy Woollen District and the *Dewsbury Reporter* has been its newspaper for over a century. It began life in August 1858, a venture of the Woodhead family of Huddersfield, proprietors of the *Huddersfield Examiner*. Local pride however could not endlessly endure the thought that the local paper was distantly owned and printed, and in 1897, a group of Liberals in Dewsbury asserted themselves. Either the Woodheads would sell them the *Reporter* or they would start their own Dewsbury newspaper. They got the *Reporter* and formed a company to run it, The Reporter Ltd. Every shareholder had to

The reporting staff at the *Dewsbury Reporter*—March, 1897

sign a declaration that he was a supporter of Liberal principles.

Partisan fervour usually ends in journalistic failure, but the *Dewsbury Reporter* seems to be the exception that proves the rule. Unflagging advocacy of Liberalism has gone hand in hand with handsome commercial success. At times the paper has been hotly aggressive in furthering its cause, as when it had to pay damages to a political opponent for calling him a 'petty-fogging little attorney from Leeds'. While endeavouring to avoid similar excesses, the *Dewsbury Reporter* continues to follow its Liberal destiny under the wing of United.

Apart from politics it has always been run on highly efficient lines as a newspaper, and with business acumen by the shrewd West Riding men who have owned it. It covers every local event with scrupulous diligence. Past proprietors like the Stubleys, the Taylors and the Walkers, have known their people and their requirements. Its chairmen have been blest with long life, typifying durable qualities. Mr Theodore C. Taylor, for many years a Liberal M.P., was still active in business up to his death at the age of 102, and Sir Ronald Walker, one-time president of the national Liberal Party Organisation, who was the chairman when the property passed to United, was in his nineties when he died soon afterwards.

Among notable editors of the *Dewsbury Reporter* was Mr Oswald Jones (1906-1946), an eloquent writer who exercised remarkable influence. His Party zeal was such that more than once his paper was publicly burned by angry opponents. Mr Bernard Kaye, who occupied the chair of the *Yorkshire Evening News* when it ceased publication, returned to his native town to conduct its paper. He has now retired after long and honourable service. The present editor is Mr Jack Gowers.

At Dewsbury there is also published the *Mirfield Reporter and District News* (founded 1882).

The *Dewsbury Reporter*, 1974

FIREPLACES ! !
HEATING APPLIANCES
Easy Terms
The Batley Barless
Fire Co. Limited
HICK LANE JUNCTION
Hours 9 a.m. to 6 p.m.
Daily telephone 472297

BATLEY NEWS

Est. 1879   THURSDAY· OCTOBER 3· 1974   Price 4p

1974

Batley News and Reporter
WHEN THE MANGLE CRASHED

Batley lies very close to Dewsbury and though Dewsbury claims to derive its name from the Latin equivalent of 'God's Borough' Batley has never conceded any divine authority to its neighbour. Since October 1879 it has had its own paper, begun as the *Batley News*. Not only does it emphasise its independence of things purely Dewsburian but it has earned a national reputation as a training paper for journalists. This is due to the outstanding ability and tremendous drive of Mr Rayner Roberts, who was editor-proprietor from 1902 until his death in 1942.

The *Batley News* was founded by a barber's apprentice named James Fearnsides. His editorial staff consisted of a compositor from a music printing works who knew more about crotchets and quavers than he did about reporting, and altogether it was an amateur affair for some years. Up to 1894 it ambled along without any type-setting machinery and without a telephone.

The paper then passed successively through the hands of Mr P. D. McGowan and Mr F. H. Purchas before the energetic Rayner Roberts got hold of it. He changed everything. He was a titan for work, putting in 80 hours a week and demanding such exertions from his subordinates that many of them could not stick it. They came and they went, but those who stayed learnt their craft thoroughly and a dozen or so of Rayner Roberts' 'boys' subsequently became editors of newspapers.

He had to fight formidable competition from the richer *Batley Reporter*, an offshoot of the *Dewsbury Reporter*, which often carried twice as many pages as the *News*. Nevertheless people preferred the *News* and its sale in Batley forged ahead. In 1959 however it was taken over by The Reporter Ltd., the board of which was joined by Rayner Roberts' daughter, Miss G. M. R. Roberts, and Mr Derrick Boothroyd, who at that time was editing the paper.

There are still some who remember a hectic event in the history of the *Batley News*. It occurred in 1926. Part of the office was wrecked by a gas explosion—on the very eve of publication. The

159

old flong mangle crashed through the floor into the accounts department below. Promptly the *Dewsbury Reporter* offered to help, and all through the night Rayner Roberts, wearing the white tie and tails he had donned for a public function that evening, was to be seen in the *Reporter* office poring over inky formes, putting his paper to bed with metal supplied by his competitor. His successor today is Mr Keith Hustler.

Papers associated with the *Batley News* are the localised edition, *Birstall News* (launched in 1880) and the admirable weekly which for just over a hundred years has served the people of nearby Morley.

Morley Observer
'WE'RE ALL RIGHT'
An attractive and highly prosperous town, Morley lies to the north of Batley. In the vicinity are some fine specimens of West Riding domestic architecture; among these the town cherishes the birthplace of its most famous son, H. H. Asquith, Prime Minister and later Lord Oxford and Asquith.

Morley has always, and rightly, maintained its independence of the encroaching pressures of the city of Leeds. Today its survival as a separate community has to be maintained in spite of changes in local government. The battle is being led by the *Morley Observer*. Whatever has happened in the way of technical administration, Morley will continue to exert its own view, and foster its own traditions, with the *Morley Observer* as its journalistic mouthpiece. 'We're all right, it's t'other folk that's queer', said a recent significant headline.

The paper celebrated its centenary in 1971. It was first published on Saturday October 7 1871 as the *Morley Observer and Gildersome, Drighlington, Adwalton, Churwell and Ardsley Advertiser*. Mr Samuel Stead, a personification of Victorian integrity and loftiness of purpose, was the publisher, and the paper continued to be owned by the Stead family until the late 1950s. Grandsons of the founder, Mr Henry Stead and his brother George, were in control when it then became vested in the *Batley News* ownership which, as already explained, later merged with The Reporter Ltd., of Dewsbury.

Unlike the *Dewsbury Reporter* the *Morley Observer* is not

MORLEY MOTORS		HAINSWORTH
LIMITED		The Jeweller
Specialised		WINDSOR COURT
B.M.C.		MORLEY
SALES and SERVICE		Telephone 2713
Ring Morley 4333		Repairs Established
anytime		same day 100 years

MORLEY OBSERVER

Est. 1871   THURSDAY. OCTOBER 3. 1974   Price 4p

1974

committed to political partisanship. It stands for Morley—all the people of Morley. In his first editorial old Samuel Stead set the sights: 'We care not to ape an infallibility which is denied to mankind. But at least we pledge ourselves to honesty and single-ness of purpose. We wish the truth to be stated in these columns without fear or favour, and to hold the balance evenly between contending parties.'

Goole Times

NEVER GIVE A BOY A SHILLING...

On August 1 1853 the *Goole Times* arrived on the scene with a front-page leading article headlined 'Here We Are!' That was a startlingly crisp headline to offer sedate Victorian readers, and the short leader itself was written in the same vein: 'Our plan is to furnished in as brief a form as possible the most important intelligence of the past month, and a very concise Parliamentary summary which we imagine will be far more acceptable than full reports of prosy debates.'

This indicated that the newspaper was not going to be either pretentious or verbose. Nor has it ever been; it is a down-to-earth comprehensive weekly newspaper, unafflicted with ideology, concerned all the time about what goes on in its thriving town and seaport.

Goole had a population of 450 in 1821, 5,000 in the year the *Goole Times* was founded, 16,000 at the beginning of this century, and around 19,000 today, and the *Goole Times* goes into most of its homes.

It was started as a monthly by John Kay, a printer and stationer who was also 'keeper' of the Post Office; but when George Sutton arrived in the town and took it over—after experience on the *Doncaster Gazette*—he promptly switched to weekly publication and gave it the impetus that ensured success. Later it came under the control of Mr H. T. Gardiner, an experienced journalist, who eventually sold out to the Goole Times Co. in the 1890s. Now-adays, while admirably edited by Mr E. Butler and his young staff at Goole, it is printed along with the *Driffield Times*.

Goole lies on the Yorkshire Ouse some fifty miles from the North Sea but it is a port of much consequence, carrying on a lively trade between the industrial West Riding and northern Europe—a trade which looks like developing apace. Shipbuilding is also one of the town's activities, and the river, the docks and the yards have commanded watchful attention from the *Goole Times* for well over a hundred years.

With a Humber bridge now going ahead it is interesting to recall how the *Times* was in the van of a great protest against a similar scheme years ago. Goole 'rose in arms' and the battle to stop the estuary bridge occupied nearly a month of argument in committee rooms of the House of Commons. Sea captains who had long navigated the Ouse and Humber were among scores of witnesses at the inquiry.

Files of the *Goole Times* faithfully record the changing life of its river; they include an account of a cricket match played on it when the port was frozen up in 1879.

A peculiar kind of whimsy seems to have characterised its first editor. Here are specimens of advice given to his 'gentle readers':

How to become wise?—Eat, sleep and say nothing.

How to become slandered?—Edit a paper and tell the truth.

Never give a boy a shilling to hold your shadow while you climb a tree to look into the middle of next week; it is money thrown away.

As far back as the days of George Sutton the *Goole Times* began to publish local editions, the *Howdenshire Gazette* and the *Selby Express*. These are now combined in the *Gazette*.

Mastheads of the *Goole Times* and *Howdenshire Gazette*, 1974

Driffield Times mastheads of 1860 and 1974

Driffield Times

ROMANCE OF THE ERRAND BOY

When the eye scans the front page of the first issue of the *Driffield Times* (January 21 1860) it dilates with a wild surmise. For there, in prominent type, is an advertisement for 'Crippen's Sufferer's Friend'. Unlike his celebrated namesake however this Mr Crippen of Nafferton village was not apparently a qualified physician, although 'eruptions of every description' did not daunt him any more than did 'bad legs of many years standing'.

Otherwise that edition was a dignified newspaper containing a wealth of local news. Addressed to the inhabitants of a great agricultural area of the East Riding, it provided much information for the farmer and his wife, as it does today.

The paper was founded by George Robert Jackson, a native of Sledmere. He served his apprenticeship as a printer in Driffield before setting up on his own account. An enterprising young man, he installed 'the most modern newspaper press of the day' to print the *Driffield Times*, a press that became historic. It was called a Caxton and it was 'calculated to work a newspaper without risk of breaking down'—an assurance which some contemporary machine room staffs will note with envy. At first it was worked by hand, but in 1865 the *Driffield Times* was able to set at its masthead the words 'Printed by Steam Power'. As a matter of fact that original Caxton press produced the paper until February 1922, when it was the oldest representative of its breed still functioning in England.

Since the day it was born the *Driffield Times* has served the community of the Yorkshire Wolds with steadfast application. Farming, breeding—especially horses and sheep—cricket, village shows, days out with the Middleton or Holderness hounds—these

163

are the stuff of its life now as they were in 1860. The paper had a number of proprietors—at one time a Congregational minister was its chairman—before it came into the hands of Yorkshire Post Newspapers and eventually under the umbrella of United.

Proprietors indeed have been more transient than staff, for the *Times* has a proud record of long service. Most remarkable was that of Mr J. E. Hart. He joined the paper as an errand boy in 1897, ultimately became its editor, and was still in the chair when it celebrated its centenary in 1960, sixty-three years later.

Mr Hart, like his predecessors and successors, exercised a steady influence on the life of the area. The *Driffield Times* has a point of view and is not reticent in stating it, though nowadays it is usually more explicit than it was in its first issue. Then it upbraided the local youth for being apathetic towards the Volunteer Rifle Corps—

> Our young men must be degenerate sons of a nobler race. They do not display the pluck and spirit which animated their sires when they went to Burlington (Bridlington) to meet Napoleon I, intending to give him a warm reception and with the certain prospect of immediate destruction before them.

There is something in that passage which seems to defeat its purpose; the final words suggest that the Driffield lads of 1860 were not so daft as their over-zealous grandparents.

The *Driffield Times* which is well-edited today by Mr John Barrett, has associated papers serving Beverley and Pocklington.

Pocklington Times

THE HYMN WE LOVE

Amid tranquil pastoral scenery where the Vale of York begins to lift itself to the Wolds you find the small market town of Pocklington. It has plenty of work to do, work deriving greatly from agriculture, and it likes to go its own quiet way without bothering anybody else. For this disposition the *Pocklington Times*

Masthead of the *Pocklington Times*, 1974

ESTIMATES FREE
BEAVERCRAFT
A. Wilson N.I.C.E.I.
Electrical Contractors

HOOVER SERVICE
by
Ex-Hoover Representative

22 North Bar Within
Beverley. Tel. 882058
Private Phone 884254

BEVERLEY GUARDIAN

TELEPHONE BEVERLEY 882111   Editorial and Advertisement Offices: 8 Market Place, Beverley   TELEPHONE BEVERLEY 882111

No. 6174   THURSDAY, 3rd OCTOBER, 1974   Price 4p

Used Cars
consult
Thompson
of
Beverley Ltd.
SWINEMOOR LANE
Telephone 882217

Masthead of the *Beverley Guardian*, 1974

caters week by week and the inhabitants read it and help along its activities; a little paper, a localised edition of the *Driffield Times*, giving a little town something of its own in print.

The *Pocklington Times* does not make a noise in the world, nor does Pocklington town, but the wayfarer may pause a moment when he reflects that the Rev. Clement Scholefield went to Pocklington School—the man who composed the beautiful tune to which we sing *The Day Thou Gavest, Lord, is Ended*, recently voted 'top of the pops' in hymnology.

Beverley Guardian

WHODUNWOT?

If your bias is toward a contemplative life in an old town setting you could not do better than hie you to Beverley. Beverley Minster—a medieval prayer realised in stone—and St Mary's Church with its famous flying buttresses are among Christendom's most exquisite monuments. They dominate a town of narrow ways, pantiled cottages and Georgian houses gathered around a broad market place.

Moreover, should you by some remote chance be also disposed toward domestic service, you could do worse than go to Beverley. In 1862, a Mr Matthew Turner, provoked into prodigality by the perpetual comings and goings of his household staff, endowed a charity out of which faithful servants were to be rewarded. Ten pounds used to be given to each of some twenty competitors: today, like so many other things, it has gotten itself inflated and is now £20; and its administration is duly reported in the town's newspaper, the *Beverley Guardian*.

The *Guardian* first came out on January 5 1856, the venture of John Green & Co., stationers and printers, in the Market Place. The firm of Green still exists but no longer owns the paper, which passed through the hands of Wright and Hoggard into those of East Yorkshire Printers of Driffield and thence into the United commonwealth.

For many years the sheets, printed on a flatbed machine, were sent from the printing works on the outskirts of the town to the Green premises two miles away, where they were folded and packed under the supervision of one Ted Vickerman who had worked for the firm for over sixty years as a bookbinder.

As the present editor says, the *Beverley Guardian* does not offer a sensationally new look, but neither does Beverley itself, and that is one reason why the people like it, for its service of news and views continues to present that 'honest record of passing events' which the founders promised at the outset. Such honesty however can sometimes be a trifle imprecise. There is an item in the file of November 20 1869 which seems to leave everything hanging in the air; not so much whodunit? as whodunwot?

Fatal Affray at Bishop Burton

On Tuesday night the inhabitants of this quiet village, soon after they had retired to rest, were thrown into the greatest consternation and excitement owing to a serious calamity which befell the head gamekeeper, John Washington Jex, the under-keeper, William Geddes, and Mark Robinson, a watcher, in the service of Richard Watt, Esq., the former, melancholy to relate, having come to an untimely end and having been killed on the spot.

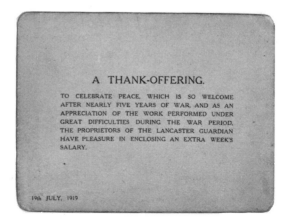

A THANK-OFFERING.

TO CELEBRATE PEACE, WHICH IS SO WELCOME AFTER NEARLY FIVE YEARS OF WAR, AND AS AN APPRECIATION OF THE WORK PERFORMED UNDER GREAT DIFFICULTIES DURING THE WAR PERIOD, THE PROPRIETORS OF THE LANCASTER GUARDIAN HAVE PLEASURE IN ENCLOSING AN EXTRA WEEK'S SALARY.

19th JULY, 1919

7

PUNCH

A PROPHETIC sentence ends *A History of Punch*, by Mr R. G. G. Price, published in 1957—'*Punch's* future is more interesting than its past'. The last five years have wholly justified Mr Price's perception, for *Punch* has renewed itself in a fashion that has made it a vivid microcosm of the extraordinary world of today—a world which, bewildering as it is to all of us by the rapidity of its change, stands remote from the equable society of yesterday with which *Punch* came to be associated.

Although in fact *Punch* has always moved with the times, its duty as a comic and satiric mirror of the passing scene constrains it to move with the precise pace of 'the times', neither voyaging ahead nor stumbling behind. During the past decade the pace has been so fast, the transformation of scene and poise so dramatic, that *Punch* had either to 'get a move on' such as it had never had to do in all its previous life, or become a drop-out.

That was the situation confronting it when United Newspapers acquired Bradbury Agnew in 1969. It was trying to 'get a move on' but was unsure of itself and flagging. The business was carrying a load of mounting costs and other difficulties. What was to be done about *Punch* in this generation of affluence, permissiveness, porn, demo, women's lib and LSD? Could it breathe in such a climate—*Punch*, that had been the dear repository of homespun humour, that had amused domestic firesides with its vicars and teacups, old ladies and tramps, and, in sterner mood, inspired us with cartoon assertions of principles and practices now, like Empire, dissolving in our Century of the Common Man?

Admittedly the old gentleman had a wealth of experience and a shrewdness of eye and mind for the things around him; but was he capable of jumping into this maelstrom without looking like a Norfolk-jacketed has-been amid the jeans and leathers? Some felt the feat to be impossible and that he should confine himself to nourishing the nostalgia of other old ladies and gentlemen. But where would this lead in the end other than to a grave, dug in the waiting rooms of Harley Street consultants and provincial dentists?

Fortunately other views prevailed and another faith was proclaimed. Sir William Barnetson took a tenacious grip of *Punch*, working closely with Mr Victor Caudery, the managing director, and with Mr William Davis, the editor. If it entered the times boldly *Punch* could be entirely identified with them, and what was more it could be made to pay.

The key to success, as ever in the case of Barnetson, was selection and simplification. For *Punch* or any other single medium to reflect, week by week, the whole spectrum of a living scene that had multiplied its aspects so prodigiously was impossible. Take one thing at a time. He encouraged Davis further to exploit what he had begun—a weekly theme, one week the monarchy, another week the tycoon, another the package tour, the motorist, or the Pope and his Vatican. Even the playboy, with accompanying boudoir of bosoms, bottoms and porn was given a week's satiric airing.

And success *has* come. *Punch* now belongs to the 'seventies; along with the younger generation it has carried other old gentlemen with it, is enjoying itself, and is making money. If it doesn't look like what it looked when we were young it is nevertheless the same clever and engaging friend. It may be dressed in new clothes—who isn't?—and it uses another idiom—who doesn't?—but it still prods the ribs of mankind with its traditional weapons of good and witty writing and the best cartoons that the best artists of the day can provide.

All over the globe, too, there is a keen revival of interest in *Punch* as a British institution and as the world medium *par excellence* for the highest quality advertising. That advertising now enjoys first-class colour printing.

It was on Saturday July 17 1841 that *Punch* came out into a London buzzing with short-lived periodicals, some scurrilous, some politically bitter, some comic. The idea that the figure of Mr Punch (the husband of Mistress Judy) was a proper symbol for journalistic fun and irony had been tried out more than once. There was a paper called *Punchinello* and Douglas Jerrold ran one called *Punch in London*. They did not endure. The one that was content to call itself simply *Punch*, 'a new work of wit and whim', has endured for over 130 years.

Who actually instigated it nobody quite knows. Two men who did the job of bringing it out were Ebenezer Landells, an engraver, and Henry Mayhew, a journalist. Presently it was revealed that the property named *Punch* was divided as to two thirds between Landells and a printer, Joseph Last, and as to one third between Mayhew, Mark Lemon, and Stirling Coyne, who called themselves co-editors.

In the event Mark Lemon emerged as the prevailing editor. He was an ill-educated hack writer of Jewish origin, but he became the man who gave *Punch* its original mixture of broad fun and biting comment illustrated by little black-and-white cuts. Lemon was a chap bursting with high spirits and tavern foolery; he drew from Hans Andersen the remark, 'Mr Lemon is most excellent full of comic'.

But *Punch* lost money and in December 1842 Bradbury and Evans (publishers of some of the novels of Dickens and Thackeray) took it over with the assistance of Mark Lemon and Douglas Jerrold, who had become its principal writer. Thackeray also wrote for the paper under the pseudonym 'Our Fat Contributor' and exerted an influence upon its content. He drew his own sketches to illustrate his own articles.

The famous *Punch* Table was founded in those earliest years. Nowadays it is a luncheon gathering but it was originally a dinner table round which the proprietors, the editor, the staff and distinguished contributors assembled to discuss what they should do with pending issues. Argument was sometimes ferocious and laughter generally hilarious as the wine went round. Gradually a tradition was established by which the elite of the Table carved their initials into its hefty deal, and today it is a unique 'autograph album' of world-famous artists and writers.

An early photograph of *Punch* staff and contributors at the famous table

Punch has never been 'non-political'; neither has it been consistent in its opinions. In turn it has been Radical and Tory. During one period it was notorious for its pungent satire at the expense of the Royal Family. It has been vulgar and respectable, crude and genteel, orthodox and aberrant. Sometimes it has lost its way and vitality has diminished; sometimes it has had joyous spurts of genius and popularity. But *Punch* would cease to be *Punch* if it allowed its vein of compassion to atrophy—compassion for the rejected, the oppressed, the tyrannised.

Tom Hood's pathetic *Song of the Shirt* was first published in *Punch*. Mark Lemon printed it despite the unanimous and vociferous opposition of his staff. It was in fact this single poem, which appeared at Christmas 1843, that first brought *Punch* its

international fame and established Lemon as a great editor—for in
the last resort an editor must be an autocrat or quit.

> *With fingers weary and worn,*
> *With eyelids heavy and red,*
> *A Woman sat in unwomanly rags,*
> *Plying her needle and thread—*
> *Stitch! Stitch! Stitch!*
> *In poverty hunger and dirt,*
> *And still with a voice of dolorous pitch*
> *She sang the 'Song of the Shirt'.*

Altogether there have been ten editors of *Punch*. After Mark
Lemon came Shirley Brooks (1870-1874), a notable wit and
graceful writer who is credited with the saying, 'The love of evil
is the root of all money.' He was followed by a more plodding
type, Tom Taylor, who made *Punch* a little too respectable.
During Sir Francis Burnand's long spell in the chair (1880-1906)
new liveliness and plenty of robust laughter came back. He was
a playright and cared little for politics. There was a time when
he and his friend W. S. Gilbert found themselves at loggerheads.
Happening to meet Gilbert at a dinner party, Burnand remarked,
'All the good things are sent in to *Punch*.'

'Then why don't you put them in your paper?' retorted Gilbert.

Sir Owen Seaman, a scholar and master of parody, was editor
from 1906 to 1932. He was not a great innovator but he kept the
quality and detail of the paper at a very high level, and it lay
ready for the brisker, more modern, humour of E. V. Knox
('Evoe') when he succeeded. Knox, another gifted parodist,
tightened up the features and captions and allowed the new kind
of 'shaggy dog' joke to appear.

Kenneth Bird ('Fougasse') was the first artist to become editor
of *Punch*. For three years he made a very good job of it before
returning to the drawing board and making way for Malcolm
Muggeridge. Muggeridge was a newspaper journalist and broadcaster, best known today for his television work and religious
advocacy. He edited *Punch* from 1953 to 1957 and focused much
attention by his outspoken comment; if he irritated some readers
he made them aware of the paper's existence and vigour. In
choosing a successor the proprietors went back to form. Bernard
Hollowood had been a contributor of articles and sketches for

more than a decade. As editor he restored more of the original fun and games, at the same time maintaining the Muggeridge view that *Punch* should be politically recognised.

William Davis has been in the chair for six years, having taken over from Hollowood in 1969. Until then his experience had been in financial journalism; he was in turn City editor of the *Evening Standard* and financial editor of the *Guardian*. He has a fertility of mind and a liveliness of manner that create a sense of breathlessness. He talks like a 'demo'—the pressure of ideas in the rearguard seems continually to be overtaking those proclaimed in the van.

Nowadays editors of periodicals and newspapers alike are prone to become identifiable public figures but it remains true that their real business is to be felt rather than seen—felt through the character of their papers and the genius of the men and women they select to fill their columns. People think of *Punch* in terms of the famous writers and artists who have been associated with it rather than in terms of those who have edited it. What a galaxy they present!

The artists and cartoonists deserve pride of place. They ring the memory in splendid procession—Dickens' Phiz, John Leech, Richard Doyle, Sir John Tenniel (whose 'Dropping the Pilot' is probably the most famous of all political cartoons), George du Maurier and his fantasies, the immortal Phil May, Harry Furniss, Frank Reynolds, Bernard Partridge, H. M. Bateman, E. H. Shepard, George Belcher, Fougasse, David Langdon, Illingworth, Emmet, Ronald Searle, Thelwell, Mahood, ffolkes and Trog.

The cream of British black-and-white work is to be found in the volumes of *Punch* Some of the captions have passed into the language. There was the old man who told the visiting lady what he did with his time: 'Well mum, sometimes I sits and thinks, and then again I just sits.' The 'curate's egg' joke was a du Maurier caption published in 1895. 'I'm afraid you've got a bad egg, Mr Jones', said the bishop. 'Oh no, my Lord', replied Mr Jones, 'I assure you, parts of it are excellent.'

Lots of *Punch* quips have attained a similar immortality. Many phrases that come readily to the tongue were first printed in its pages, like 'Bang went saxpence' (1868), the tramp and his soap testimonial, 'since then I have used no other' (1884), 'Feed the

TRUE HUMILITY.

Right Reverend Host. "I 'M AFRAID YOU 'VE GOT A BAD EGG, MR. JONES!"
The Curate. "OH NO, MY LORD, I ASSURE YOU! PARTS OF IT ARE EXCELLENT!"

'The Curate's Egg'—from *Punch* (1895)

brute' (1883), 'I don't mind if I do' (1900), 'It's only us keeping so cheerful as pulls us through' (1916). And, of course, most celebrated of all, Mr Punch's advice to persons about to marry, *Don't*. It appeared in the *Punch* Almanac for 1845, a bit of Mark Lemonism. Limericks have included that choice specimen, 'There was a Young Lady of Gloucester—'

Of writers, down from the time of Thackeray to the present, most whose genius has shone brightly through the amusing or ironic have contributed to *Punch* either in prose or verse. The humour of men like F. Anstey (*Vice Versa*) belongs to another age, but one has only to think of modern contributors to realise what a fund of excellent light literature is enfolded in the *Punch* files.

Sir Alan Herbert adorned its pages for many years; one could hardly imagine *Punch* without A.P.H. Then there were 'Evoe', A. A. Milne and E. V. Lucas to charm us, and Anthony Armstrong, P. G. Wodehouse (briefly), Hugh Kingsmill and John Betjeman. Today Alan Coren, Basil Boothroyd, Miles Kington and others continue the tradition.

So comprehensive is the list that one is driven to look for omissions. If only Charles Lamb had lived a little longer how ideally he would have fitted into *Punch*! That could not be

The Chairman of United Newspapers welcomes Mr Edward Heath arriving for a *Punch* luncheon

Mr Harold Wilson sits between Mr William Davis, Editor of *Punch* (right), and Mr Alan Coren, Deputy Editor, at one of the weekly lunches

helped, but what about Dickens? Nothing of his appeared but he did submit a contribution and it was rejected. Alas! every editor is unpleasantly conscious of some decision he does not like to remember.

Rejections have also had to be made, often reluctantly, in deference to prevailing taste. Among newspaper cuttings sent in by readers but at the time deemed too *risque* to publish were these:

Mrs Winston Churchill told members of Y.W.C.A. committees in Liverpool recently, 'Ninety per cent of the mistresses in Y.W.C.A. hostel beds are not fit to sleep on. They are lumpy and uncomfortable.'

Two attractive young ladies would like to meet two tall gentlemen with cars and things. Sincere. Box K 277.

Editor William Davis takes Mr Punch from Bouverie Street to its new home at Tudor Street, headquarters of United Newspapers

When United Newspapers acquired *Punch* in 1969 it was a revolutionary change in proprietorship, for since 1842 it had been conducted by what was, in essence, the same family business. Bradbury Evans & Co. continued as such until 1865. Then the house of Agnew, the art dealers, became associated with it. Seven years later, when Mr F. M. Evans left the firm the name was changed to Bradbury Agnew & Co. under which it traded up to the time of the deal with United. Mr Peter Agnew, though no longer occupied with executive work, remains on the board of Bradbury Agnew, a happy maintenance of family tradition.

During the first few years of its life *Punch* was published at Crane Court, Fleet Street, but when Bradbury Evans took over it was administered from their office in Bouverie Street. There it remained throughout the Bradbury Agnew regime, the large effigy of Mr Punch over the doorway being a familiar sight to more than one generation of passers-by. There was inevitable sadness on the day when the effigy was taken down and removed to the entrance hall of United Newspapers round the corner in Tudor Street, but economies were imperative and the old building had to be sold. It was bought by Lord Rothermere's Associated Newspapers.

Yet even in the brief years that have passed since then it has become obvious that Mr Punch likes his new home and his new friends. They are determined that he shall thrive, accoutred with all his old 'regalia', enjoying his old mode of life. The Table now stands in a special *Punch* room at Tudor Street. Distinguished guests, who have included Prince Charles, are entertained there by the fraternity. Every Wednesday the weekly luncheon takes place as in the days of yore, and the laughter and backchat are what they were when Thackeray and 'Phiz' contributed.

On the surrounding walls are pictures of every man who has been 'on the Table' since the beginning. Drawings by Sir John Tenniel and Sir Bernard Partridge are there among a priceless collection of other cartoons. There also is Mark Lemon's original handwritten prospectus for *Punch*.

COUNTRY LIVING

NEWSPAPER managers may cherish the friendship of their journalistic colleagues but they regard them (generally with justification) as hopelessly unrealistic when it comes to business matters. In the same way journalists are apt to consider their managers as deplorably unimaginative, ridiculously anchored to economic theory. On just a few occasions the journalists have proved their case, and *The Countryman* is the outstanding example.

When Robertson Scott decided to launch *The Countryman* in 1927 he was given dire warnings by marketing experts. He was told that quarterlies were out of date, his proposed price and size impossible, short articles a handicap, and advertisers reluctant. Nevertheless he went ahead. His capital was £200—laughably inadequate by accepted standards—but he spent it on a pocket-size, elegantly printed magazine of 82 editorial pages and sixteen pages of advertising, selling at the then preposterous price of half a crown. It never looked back.

Seven years later *The Countryman* consisted of 162 editorial pages and 184 advertisement pages and its circulation was over 8,000. Today it sells nearly 70,000 copies every quarter and has readers in every part of the world, recent letters testifying to their existence in places as far apart as Addis Ababa and Venezuela.

In his autobiography Robertson Scott defines the aims he had in view.

> This *Countryman* would be . . . half a crown, and for the country dweller devoted to rural life and for the townsman and townswoman who only wished they could live in the country too; pocket size; at least a

hundred pages; typographically comely; at a high level in illustrations; wholly produced in the country—indeed, except for the printing, in my house; published no more often than once a quarter; non-Party though sturdy enough in opinion; packed with rural life and character, human and bird and beast; writing of the very best, and scenery without gush or twaddle; reinforcing and co-ordinating the force of rural progress and throwing light on the path the forward movement was taking and ought to take; presenting in a brisk way the constructive thought of fertile and penetrating minds; stimulating candid discussion; placing before town, city and country dwellers vividly and convincingly an intelligent view; and above all, worthy of the attention and confidence of cultivated people.

A lot of semi-colons in that, but throughout the 48 years which have passed since its foundation those who have been responsible for *The Countryman* have never deviated from the principles they enclose, and those principles are being pursued with energy and success under the wing of United. Within the familiar green covers readers find writing and thought of the quality which Robertson Scott insisted on from the first, illustrations that appeal to the discriminating mind, and paper and typography that satisfy the discerning eye.

There is nothing like *The Countryman*; it is unique. Its readers are the most loyal in the world for it has become an institution without which country living would lose much of its savour. Its arrival every quarter in manor and cottage and farm—and in many a city home where there is love of the country—is an event which deepens the season's character and heightens the season's colour. And there is so much in it—long hours of reading over the fire in winter, substance for meditation amid the June-high grasses.

Robertson Scott was sixty years old when he started *The Countryman*. He sensed his public accurately in spite of the head-shaking of the 'experts', and his timing turned out to have been shrewd. For many years agriculture had been depressed but revitalisation came in the 1930s. Also a new kind of countryman was emerging. As the present editor writes, 'The move of the

The editor of *The Countryman* at work in his garden at Burford

better-off townsman to country houses that had begun in the last quarter of the nineteenth century with the increased mobility given by the railways, was increased enormously with the advent of the cheap motor-car. The neo-Georgian writers were extolling the joys of village cricket matches and walks over the Downs; rustic life was fashionable and the vanishing country crafts and characters becoming as exotic as did steam locomotives in their last years'. To this one may add that, thanks to *The Countryman* and what it stands for, many country crafts are now renewing themselves and lending grace to our otherwise rather shabby civilisation.

At the beginning *The Countryman* came from Idbury Manor, Robertson Scott's home in a Cotswold village between Burford and Bourton-on-the-Water. His small staff tackled everything, including the wrapping of postal copies. He continued as editor, publisher, manager and absolute dictator until he was 80. His wife was his partner and assistant editor. But the time came when they both decided that they needed a peaceful home in which to spend their declining years, and the ownership and business management of the magazine was sold to Bradbury Agnew. Editorial control remained with Robertson Scott and his successors.

When Robertson Scott retired a farewell luncheon was held round the *Punch* table, the guests including the then Prime Minister, Clement Attlee, and that literary soldier Field Marshal Lord Wavell.

Mr John Cripps, a son of Sir Stafford, who had first joined *The Countryman* as advertisement manager and had become Robertson Scott's right-hand man, took over the editorship. Following the founder's example he established the editorial office in a country home, Greyhounds, a Tudor house in Burford which had been a coaching inn during the eighteenth century. Its address, Sheep Street, Burford, Oxford, where it is still edited, has become as famous as the original home, Idbury Manor.

To John Cripps and his assistant editor, Mrs Faith Sharp, *The Countryman* owes much gratitude for they succeeded in the task of carrying on the traditions bequeathed by their formidable predecessor and ensured their vitality during the changing world of the 1950s and 1960s. In 1970 Cripps was appointed chairman of the Countryside Commission and in 1971, after 34 years with the magazine, he retired, though remaining a director. Mr Norman Whinfrey had been appointed chairman of *The Countryman* when Bradbury Agnew became part of United.

Crispin Gill, a West-Country journalist, succeeded John Cripps as editor and remains in the chair today. The printing of *The Countryman* went back to its original printers, the Alden Press at Oxford, and was changed from letterpress to modern lithography. Gill has also followed Robertson Scott's practice and made his home at the office in Sheep Street so that today's periodical functions in the manner prescribed for it by the remarkable man who launched it.

There is no property in the possession of United of which the company is more proud than it is of *The Countryman*.

Farmers Guardian

While *The Countryman* thus provides country lovers with a quarterly review of distinctive literary quality, other United publications are concerned with practical farming. Among them is the weekly *Farmers Guardian* which has enjoyed remarkable success and is now established in the agricultural community over a wide area of England and Wales.

Originally it was the *Preston Guardian*, the weekly newspaper on which the Toulmins founded their fortune. It continued as a general newspaper until the 1950s when it began to develop sales problems due to the effective presence of the *Lancashire Evening Post* in the same town. When the local news is printed daily a paper that only comes out once a week is inevitably handicapped.

But there was an element in the *Preston Guardian* which marked it out from other weeklies faced with a similar situation. It had always carried much information addressed to farmers in Lancashire and the districts around. Its influence as an agricultural paper was, in fact, developing though sales on the whole were falling.

A 1974 front page of the *Farmers Guardian*

A bold decision was taken. In May 1958 the *Farmers Guardian* was launched as an all-farming edition of the *Preston Guardian*. Four years later the *Preston Guardian* newspaper disappeared, its offspring, the *Farmers Guardian* having reached a condition of steady growth. By then it was selling throughout Lancashire, Cheshire and South Westmorland, and a branch office had been opened in Cheshire.

Today it has a sales structure unlike any other agricultural journal. It publishes three editions, serving the North of England, the West Midlands, and the whole of Wales, and its readership is expanding. It has won the esteem of farmers in all branches of agriculture and its technical and political influence on the industry is recognised not only in its large circulation area but at national level. The editor, Mr S. H. Seaton, enjoys a high reputation as a broadcaster as well as a writer on farming matters.

Pigs, Cows, Corn . . .

From the Farming Press at Ipswich come three monthly publications which are the 'quality' magazines of British agriculture. They are the *Dairy Farmer* (established in 1929 and edited by Mr D. Shead), *Pig Farming* (1953, editor Mr B. T. Hogley) and *Arable Farming* (1966, editor Mr G. R. Rumsey). As their titles indicate, they cater for specific fields. They are handsomely produced, excellently illustrated and highly authoritative, being edited and written by acknowledged experts. They have a particular appeal to farmers eager to keep abreast of the most modern practices. Together they represent the last word in their branch of journalism.

Their histories may not be extensive for they have come into being during an era in which farming has depended on keener and keener 'expertise'. It is that which they are intended to meet and farmers are everywhere realising how efficiently they are meeting it.

Country living may include appreciation of the swallow and its habits—with which *The Countryman* concerns itself—but it also demands attention to the byre and the binder and the feeding trough, and it is such practical, down-to-earth considerations that occupy the pages of the *Dairy Farmer*, *Arable Farming* and *Pig Farming*.

...And Men and Women

However, lest bovine or porcine preoccupations should lend a too-rural whiff to the conclusion of this survey, we may end with a touch of human elegance. United Newspapers produce one 'glossy' which is concerned with another kind of country living—the *Northampton and County Independent*.

It is a monthly record of social activities in Northamptonshire—the hunting, the dancing, the dining, the marriage-making. Here is a county not far from London yet still belonging to the shires, and the *Independent* reflects aspects of the English way and its

With which is
incorporated .
"TOWN TALK."

An Illustrated
Journal.

NO. 3, VOL. I.   JULY, 1905.   [ONE PENNY.

AN ILLUSTRATED
JOURNAL.

With which is incorporated
"TOWN TALK."

NO. 7, VOL. I.   WEEK ENDING OCTOBER 7th, 1905.   [ONE PENNY.

Early mastheads of the *Northampton Independent*

courtesies there. It covers the social round without snobbery. It prints articles of interest both to town and country dwellers—the rich and not so rich—and takes a pride in the history of Northamptonshire.

It has been doing this since 1905 and its continuing success only goes to show how durable are the domesticities and the gregarious habits of men and women despite the scene shiftings of history. The *Northampton and County Independent* is published from the office of the Northampton *Chronicle and Echo* and is edited with enterprise by Mr L. N. Warwick.

PRINTING SINCE 1788

BEFORE the acquisition of Bradbury Agnew in 1969 some of the newspapers under the control of United had general printing works, notably at Blackpool and Blackburn, but it was the Bradbury Agnew company that brought really important printing establishments into the group.

Today United Printing Services, directed by Mr Roy Fullick, has units at Bletchley, Luton, Blackpool, Blackburn, Preston and Ormskirk, and has facilities for web-offset, litho and letterpress. It has a reputation for unrivalled colour and art work and it can print anything from a visiting card to the most sumptuous illustrated volume. Week by week it is also responsible for the production of periodicals ranging from small parish magazines to big circulation publications such as *Punch* and the *British Medical Journal*.

The name Bradbury Agnew, and before it Bradbury and Evans, has been famous in 'print' since 1833 when operations began in premises at the corner of Bouverie Street, Whitefriars. The founder of the business was Thomas Bradbury who, during a long working life, together with the distinction of having established *Punch* on a sound footing, became the close friend of leading literary figures including Dickens and Thackeray. Dickens was a frequent visitor at Bradbury's office. His novels were issued in monthly parts from the Whitefriars press which also published his magazine *Household Words*—and, incidentally, the first issues of the *Daily News*, of which Dickens was the literary editor.

Mr F. M. Evans joined the firm as a partner and after Bradbury's death in 1869 two of Bradbury's sons in turn took over the reins.

In 1890 retirement terminated the Evans family association and the Agnew family replaced it. At the beginning of the present century, when Sir William Agnew was chairman, additional printing works were established at Tonbridge, largely for book production; and subsequently came the Saffron Hill premises where for a long time *Punch* and *The Countryman* were printed.

It was during the Saffron Hill days that a remarkable record in apprenticeship and service was set up at Bradbury Agnew. Mr J. M. G. Godden, now of Potters Bar, retired after 54 years on rotary work. He had 'followed in father's footsteps', father having given some 47 years service to the firm. He in turn had followed *his* father, the first Godden having started in the machine room in 1854. What is more, the present Mr Godden's son also became apprenticed to the company, carrying the tradition into the fourth generation. Indentures covering the whole period of 120 years are prized by the family.

Changes in printing techniques and the general development of the business led to further investment and in 1951 a controlling interest in the Leagrave Press at Luton was secured. The Leagrave Press, which takes its name from marshland round the source of the River Lea, a stone's throw from the works, was founded in 1902 as Gibbs, Bamforth & Co. (Luton) Ltd., an offshoot of the *Luton News*. It became widely known for fine letterpress printing and over the years developed from its original intention, that of serving local needs, into a company with a national reputation not only in letterpress but in the field of modern colour work.

The Leagrave Press had its particular part to play in defeating Hitler; it was mainly occupied after 1939 in work for the Political Intelligence Department of the Foreign Office, producing publications in foreign languages—'psychological warfare'.

The last, and most important, venture of Bradbury Agnew before joining United was to take over George Pulman & Sons, of Bletchley. This is a name that stands high in the annals of English printing, and never higher than today, for the work which Pulman's produce is no small contribution to the renown enjoyed by United Printing Services.

It was in 1788 that a journeyman printer, Thomas Pulman, set about his ambition to become a first-rate craftsman. He had only modest equipment near Marylebone Gardens in London, but he had before him the example of that great Eighteenth Century master, John Baskerville. He laid the foundations of a business which has never deviated from his ideal—to make quality and typographical fitness the objects of endeavour. Pulmans have never been content just to feed sheets into machinery; they have never lost sight of the fact that printing is a craft which, whatever the marvels of modern technology, ceases to satisfy if it becomes a mere 'production line' affair.

Thomas Pulman the first was succeeded by Thomas the second who lived until 1864. The family continued to run the business through successive generations, right up to its coming under the umbrella of United. As printing practices developed and the market changed with the changing needs of society they continued to employ typographers and artists of distinction. Claud Lovat Fraser was among the artists who contributed 'decorations' for Pulmans. They exploited the use of good type, effective layout and colour in the field of advertising.

In the 1960s it was decided to embrace offset-litho, and Pulmans went straight into four-colour printing by this process. Expansion meant a move to larger premises and the present works, beside the Grand Union Canal at Bletchley, were acquired and equipped. In 1969 came web-offset and a new inrush of business.

Magazine work imposes the most exacting schedules and in handling some sixteen periodicals the management of Pulmans today has to exercise organisational skill. Take, for example, the sequences by which *Punch* is produced every week.

The black-and-white plates, representing 48 pages, are ready on Friday night. The colour pages which, including the cover, may range from twelve to 28, have been printed on the sheet presses during the week. As black-and-white sections come off the web press they are hurried through the Muller binding lines together with the colour sections, so that first copies of the completed *Punch* can be produced at 9.30 on Monday morning. The run continues into Tuesday and supplies are ready for despatch on the 8.30 a.m. train on Wednesday.

Into this schedule other publications have to be fitted. The *British Medical Journal*, for instance, is another big job, involving perhaps 120 pages of black-and-white plus 20 pages of colour. In this case printing begins at 6 a.m. on Wednesday, after *Punch* has been disposed of. And so on through the weeks.

General printing orders are distributed through the differing plants of United Printing Services according to their peculiar requirements. Luton may tackle one job, Blackpool another, Blackburn or Ormskirk still others.

And at Preston Mr Goward, his technical staff and his team of Lancashire lasses, handle the millions of Christmas cards that are produced there and sent off not only to customers in this country but in many parts of the world. No sooner is one Christmas over than they set about their designs, verses, and loads of sparkling 'frost' for the next. At the Castle Publishing Co. it is Christmas all the year round.

As its open printing awards testify, United Printing Services in all its branches evokes that pride in craft, that attention to detail, which epitomises true professionalism.

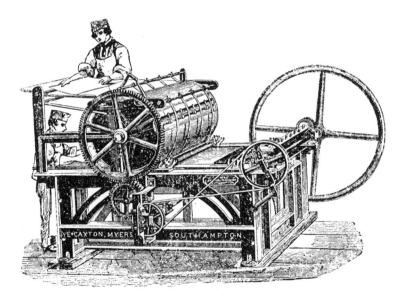

N

10

AND NOW—RADIO

WHEN you step into the entrance hall of United's headquarters at Tudor Street you will probably fail to notice a door on your right. It is a modest door with no air of consequence but it opens upon an enterprise in 'carrying the news' which is as far removed from the galloping horsemen of Northampton as is an inter-continental ballistic missile from the sling that slew Goliath.

The door leads into the Premises of Radio Fleet Productions Ltd., the most up-to-date piece of pioneering in Fleet Street.

A year or two back it became apparent that 'commercial radio', or 'independent local radio' was at last going to reach reality in Britain. Why not anticipate events by having a studio in Tudor Street that would be able to perform the same function for the sixty promised radio stations which London newspaper offices perform for their provincial newspapers? Sir William Barnetson explained his idea to the United board and the job went ahead immediately.

There was to be nothing amateurish or second-rate about the studio; it was to be equipped with the very latest instrumentation and directed by the highest professional skill available. So it is. In charge of Radio Fleet is Mr T. W. Chalmers, C.B.E., one of the best-known figures in broadcasting whose career with the B.B.C. spanned many years. Among other appointments Tom Chalmers has been Controller of the Light Programme, but he is also a technical expert and has supervised the development of Radio Fleet at every level.

Within three months the apportioned area at Tudor Street was converted into a studio, with control room, conference room, and two administrative offices. For the technically-minded let Tom Chalmers speak for himself.

'The equipment,' he writes, 'is fully stereo-capable. Its heart is a ten-channel Neve console, a small brother of the ones which the B.B.C. are installing in their London studios. Neve consoles are generally agreed to be the *ne plus ultra* of sound equipment. There are two Studer tape recorders (15 and 7½ inches per second) plus a Revox recorder/reproducer to enable copying to be done with ease and speed.

'A disc-jockey position enables a single artist to speak and operate his two Gates instant-start turntables, and to do a 'phone-in programme at the same time, though we haven't got the delay equipment that enables you to bleep-out any four-letter words your correspondent may insert—but then, neither have the B.B.C.

'A reverberation plate enables us to add echo to voices so that they sound as if they were in St Paul's Cathedral. We also have a peculiar device called a ring-modulator which we installed for the benefit of a customer who wanted to make Donald Duck and Dalek sounds. In fact, you name it; we have it. To complete the picture we added another studio on October 1 1974 to cope with all the copying and editing work we are now getting.'

Nor is Radio Fleet anchored to Tudor Street. There is a set of outside broadcasting equipment the size of a suitcase which can accommodate six microphones, and there are three Post Office lines linking the studio to the exchange at Faraday House.

What does it all do? It is not, of course, a broadcasting station; it is a feeder and servant of broadcasting. People come to Tudor Street to make recordings—to speak (or sing) solo or in a group, to engage in round-table discussions, or to prepare and tape their advertising announcements. The recordings may be broadcast from stations in Britain or overseas.

At present London has two independent radio stations— London Broadcasting and Capital Radio. It is no secret that neither had all its preparations complete when they started; consequently Radio Fleet was heavily booked for tests of staff and for pilot programmes. One such operation was a simulated phone-in programme for Capital Radio which involved the use of United's switchboard and its fifty lines.

Many firms came and recorded their commercials well in advance of 'opening day', and since then they have continued to use Radio Fleet regularly. Shift working has sometimes been necessary because London newspapers turned up at 1 a.m. to record their commercials for diffusion in the morning sessions of the London stations.

What of the future? One by one local commercial radio stations are starting to operate in cities and towns all over the country. They will require a constant flow of material from London, some of it entertainment, some commentatory—by, for example, the political correspondents of their regional newspapers—some involving debate with Members of Parliament or interviews with London executives of local industries.

Already a lot of material has been recorded that will be of interest to provincial stations, such as profiles of sporting celebrities and humorous pieces by famous *Punch* contributors. Even local B.B.C. stations have availed themselves of talks recorded by Radio Fleet.

The chances are that, should you spot a captain of industry or a T.U.C. character entering 23 Tudor Street, he will not be going to raise Cain about something that has appeared in one of United's newspapers—he will be going to talk into the microphones of Radio Fleet.

POSTSCRIPT

PRINTERS belong to a craft with many old traditions and quaint practices. One of them is called a 'Jerry'. It is simply a name for a minute or two of pandemonium in celebration of a cheerful event.

When a 'Jerry' is taking place the men seize anything that lies to hand—a length of metal rule, a hefty 'slug', a mallet—and bang it on bench or stone or chase, making a din amid which it is impossible to speak and be heard. Usually the overseer or the Father of the Chapel gives the signal to begin and end this racket.

A 'Jerry' may be invoked to mark a wedding of one of the fraternity, or a retirement, or an anniversary—anything in which the companionship takes pleasure or pride. It is a jolly affair, a letting-off of steam in the form of noise.

When I was fifteen, discovering my way on the *Leeds Mercury*, I first made acquaintance with this ritual. Always the New Year was ushered in with a 'Jerry', as it had been for a long stretch of time, for the paper was more than two hundred years old. Shortly before midnight the editor, James Lumsden, and all the editorial staff still on duty, would proceed to the case room, and the compositors, linotype operators and makers-up would cease work and gather around.

Frank Atkinson, the overseer, would watch the clock and at one minute to midnight would give the signal for the 'Jerry' to begin. The infernal noise continued until the hands of the clock had moved well past twelve. Then complete silence reigned for a moment until the principal baritone, having cleared his throat and wiped his mouth on a comparatively clean corner of his inky apron, led us all in song.

Hail smiling morn, smiling morn, smiling morn!
That tips the hills with gold—

We sang lustily, the older ones with descant acquired through repeated practice. Thus we greeted another year of promise and good fellowship. It would not have mattered if stupendous news had broken during our singing; it would have had to wait till we had gone through every verse.

Having ended this tale of United Newspapers up to the present time, I seem to hear one of those old *Leeds Mercury* 'Jerrys' and one of those old 'sings'. For they symbolised not so much the things that were gone as the things that were yet to come, and I hope that some day another hand will write another volume of this story and that the hills will continue to be 'tipped with gold' for United—not just the gold of monetary profit but also of honourable journalism.

G.S.

FINIS

A warning to City delinquents from the *Northampton Mercury*

INDEX

A

Abram, W. A., 151
Adam, Colin Forbes, 45, 46, 51, 96, 101
Advertisers' Weekly, 9
Agnew, Peter, 52, 177
Agnew, Sir William, 187
Aitken, Sir James, 154
Akerman, J. C., 8-9; vice-chairman and managing director of United Newspapers, 10, 12, 13, 17, 20, 22; F. R. Lewis and, 27, 28, 29; Drayton and, 29; resignation and death of, 34
Alden Press, Oxford, 181
Allied Newspapers, Ltd, 16, 108
Andersen, Hans, 169
Anderson, Donald, 47, 56-7
Andrews, W. Linton, 55, 96, 97-8
Anstey, F., 173
Arable Farming, 66, 183
Argus Press, 27, 43, 57
Armstrong, Anthony, 173
Askew, Barry, 123
Associated Newspapers, Ltd, 43, 177
Atkinson, Frank, 193
Attlee, Clement, 181
Austen, J. S., 31

B

Baines, Edward, 84
Baldwin, Stanley, 19, 95
Barker, Malcolm, 116
Barker, Peter, 56
Barnetson, William Denholm, 40; with *Edinburgh Evening News*, 34, 35-6, 37, 40; with United Newspapers, 38-41; in deal with Thomson, 44-5, 46; in deal with Grimes, 47, 48; succeeds Drayton as chairman (1966), 49, 50, 51, 52, 53, 54, 55, 131; knighted, 57-8; and *Punch*, 168; and Radio Fleet, 190
Barnoldswick and Earby Times, 65, 154
Barrett, John, 164
Barrons, W. Cowper, 128-9
Bateman, H. M., 172
Batley News, 57, 159-60
Batley News and Reporter, 65, 159
Batley Reporter, 159
Beckett, Hon. Rupert, 93, 96
Belcher, George, 172
Benson, G., 103-4
Betjeman, Sir John, 76, 173
Beverley Guardian, 65, 135, 165-6
Beverley sisters, Babs and Teddy, 129
Binder, Bernhard; chairman of United Newspapers, 7, 10, 11, 12, 13, 17, 50; director, 17, 18, 34, 35
Bird, Kenneth ("Fougasse"), 171, 172
Birmingham Mail, 111
Birstall News and Reporter, 65, 160
Birtill, George, 144
Blackburn Standard, 149
Blackburn Times, 7, 65, 121, 149-53
Blackburn Weekly Times, 149
Blackpool Gazette, 125, 136-8
Blackpool Gazette and Herald, 47, 65, 138-9
Blackpool Herald, 137, 138
Blackpool Times, 138
Bolton Chronicle, 119
Boothroyd, Basil, 173
Boothroyd, Derrick, 159
Bradbury, Thomas, 186